I0450132

PROPAGANDA
A QUESTION AND
ANSWER APPROACH

Henry Conserva

authorHOUSE®

AuthorHouse™
1663 Liberty Drive
Bloomington, IN 47403
www.authorhouse.com
Phone: 1-800-839-8640

© *2009 Henry Conserva. All rights reserved.*

No part of this book may be reproduced, stored in a retrieval system, or transmitted by any means without the written permission of the author.

First published by AuthorHouse 6/9/2009

ISBN: 978-1-4389-9220-4 (e)
ISBN: 978-1-4389-7441-5 (sc)
ISBN: 978-1-4389-7440-8 (hc)

Library of Congress Control Number: 2009903547

Printed in the United States of America
Bloomington, Indiana

This book is printed on acid-free paper.

ACKNOWLEDGEMENTS

I dedicate this book to my dear late wife and writing partner , Jean F. Dewees. She always encouraged me to write books for use in schools. Not only did she spend hours at a computer typing out my manuscript but offered suggestions for additions , deletions and modifications to my work. She was an author herself and co-authored *Tips for Teachers* and *Remarkable California*. As an accomplished photographer, many of her photographs have been published in a California history textbook. I treasure the memories that I have of this wonderful woman.

I'm a senior citizen who is technologically challenged by most modern devices, especially by the computer. My grandson, Geoffrey Brisson, has rescued me on several occasions and kept my book project on track. Nick Cherrill did a nice job typing the chapter on famous persuaders in world history. I'm grateful for the help given to me by Philip and Thea Conserva and Alexandra Brisson.

In doing research for my book , I was greatly aided by several librarians at the following institutions : The San Francisco Public Library System , the library at San Francisco State University and the library at Santa Rosa Junior College. I am indebted to all the professional librarians who so graciously helped me.

INTRODUCTION

Persuading people to accept our ideas and do what we want them to go is a basic universal human activity that is worth exploring.

In discussing the topic of propaganda, with teachers, students, professors and general readers, I noted that there was much confused thinking . Many people think that propaganda was always a somewhat evil activity. , the Devil's tongue as one teacher put it. Many had never heard of the existence of different forms of propaganda such as architectural propaganda , the propaganda of dress, propaganda in relation to psychological warfare, musical propaganda, propaganda in art, etc. Few people recognized advertising as a form of propaganda and the idea that propaganda was vital and necessary in every human culture was never brought up in my conversations. The idea that great religious leaders such as Jesus, Mohamud, Buddha and others were great persuaders wasn't on most people's radar screens as if the subject was taboo.

In my book I have tried to use a question and answer approach. I feel that questions are often more important than answers in getting a handle on a subject. The ten questions I chose represent just a few of the many questions that could be asked about propaganda but I hope it's a good start. The reader may want to come up with new questions and enjoy the search for answers. I enjoyed my search immensely.

As a teacher for many years , I feel that young students should be exposed to instruction in critical thinking skills to enable them to shield themselves from bad propaganda messages.

The chapter on the evolutionary history of persuasion was designed to show how human scientific and technological progress has been a very slow process of constantly increasing the reach and the speed of communication within our human family. It seems obvious that we are living at a time when progress in communication is best illustrated by a graph showing a J curve of advances in technology rapidly increasing at the end of a long period of innovational stagnation.

The bibliography has books dealing with propaganda in many historical periods in human history, many forms of propaganda and a large number of works in political propaganda. I'm hoping that this book is useful in many fields, especially in education.

CONTENTS

CHAPTER 1

WHAT TERMS SHOULD BE DEFINED IN EXPLORING THE SUBJECT?

1. Propaganda:

There are many definitions of the word propaganda. Some definitions are simple, perhaps to a fault. Other definitions are complex. Some definitions are restrictive, others more inclusive. Here a few selected definitions of propaganda.

- Propaganda is a one sided communication designed to influence peoples thinking and behavior.
- Propaganda is the art of persuasion. As a sharp knife in the hands of a skilled surgeon can save a life, in the hands of a murderer a life can be taken. Propaganda can be put to use for both good and evil purposes.
- The more or less systematic effort to manipulate other peoples beliefs, attitudes, or actions by means of symbols. We humans live in a symbolic universe.
- Propaganda includes all communications in trying to sell something. This definition would include advertising.
- Propaganda is communication who's argument relies on twisted faulty logic, misinformation, or disinformation.
- Propaganda is communication that favors emotion over reason.
- Propaganda is communication that favors belief over experience, evidence, or reason.

- Propaganda is the systematic propagation of a given doctrine or of allegations reflecting its views or interests.
- Propaganda is the manipulation of symbolic communication.
- The art of persuasion. (the authors choice)
- Propaganda is a specific type of message presentation aimed at serving an agenda. At its root, the denotation of propaganda is "to propagate (actively spread) a philosophy or point of view." the most common use of the term (historically) is in political contexts; in particular to refer to certain efforts sponsored by governments or political groups.
- Propaganda refers to any persuasive technique, whether in writing, speech, films, or other means that attempts to influence the opinions, emotions, attitudes, or behavior, of a group for the benefit of the person or organization using it. Propagandists try to put across an idea, good or bad, rather than discover the truth though reasoned argument and persuasion. The goal of a propagandist is to mold behavior to support their cause without concern for the interest or benefit of the audience.

2. White propaganda generally comes from an openly identified source, and is characterized by gentler methods of persuasion, such as standard public relations techniques and one-sided presentation of an argument.

3. Black propaganda often pretends to be from a friendly source but is actually from an adversary. Black propaganda is characterized by it's presentation of false information or elicit a desired response, and is often sued in covert military psychological operations by large networked organizations such as terror networks or governments.

4. Grey propaganda may come from an adversarial source pretending to be friendly or neutral , and presents misleading information in a more insidious manner that white propaganda. In scale these different types of propaganda can also be defined by the potential of true and correct information to complete with the propaganda. For example, opposition to white propaganda is often readily found and may slightly discredit the propaganda source.

5. Indoctrination is the teaching and acceptance of a system of thought uncritically.

6. "Brain washing" is a particular form of propaganda. The term is defined as an intensive indoctrination, usually political, aimed at changing a persons basic convictions and attitudes and replacing them with a fixed and unquestioned set of beliefs. "Brain washing" was first popularized by Edward Hunter by his 1951 book, *Brainwashing in Red China*. Brain washing was his translation for a Chinese term, "hsinao" meaning roughly "cleansing the mind". " Brain washing" was coined during the Korea war when a number of American prisoners of war violated military codes after being captured, imprisoned, interrogated, and tortured by the north Koreans and the Chinese.

7. "Spin" is the practice of interpreting statements or stories to benefit a person or group or to attack a person or group in an adversarial position. To spin is to offer a contention, usually specious, in response to a critical argument or a negative news story it does not necessarily involve lying or misleading any one about factual matters. "Spin" often but not always implies disingenuous deceptive and/or highly manipulated tactics.

8. A "spin doctor" is an advisor or a politician who interprets or slants statements or stories to the media in his or hers client's favor.

9. Enculturation is the process by which human infants learn their culture.

10. Persuasion is the act of winning over someone to a course of action by reasoning or inducement. Persuasion attempts to win "the heart and mind" of the target. Thus persuasion must induce attitude change, which entails affective (emotion-based) change .

CHAPTER 2

WHAT MAKES PEOPLE VULNERABLE TO PROPAGANDA ?

It's difficult, if not impossible, to determine what makes people vulnerable to persuasion and propaganda messages. I will indulge in speculation and list a few possible reasons for human gullibility in this matter.

- The human condition is that we are mostly ignorant about most things. Many people have trouble, from time to time, trying to figure out their own behavior. Ignorance makes us rely on faith and that opens the door to your mind from the propagandist's point of view. In my experience most political elections, religious beliefs and marriages are acts of faith. We tend to vote, pray, marry and hope for the best.
- Many people are poorly educated in most areas of knowledge and they often have deficiencies in their critical thinking skills.
- People often seem to want answers to questions that are unanswerable. The propagandist is there to provide answers he or she has chosen to promote.
- Many people are devoted to the KISS principle, (Keep It Simple Stupid). Complicated explanations are generally not popular but simple explanations and quick fixes are.
- The more the mass media resides in the hands of a few powerful individuals or corporations the easier it is to indoctrinate the masses. In a dictatorship with one party rule the government monopolizes the media. In a democracy large and wealthy corporations and

various special interest groups often try to control as much as they can of the communication industry.

- Humans have often been defined as being rational creatures. It is equally valid, in my opinion, to define humans as emotional beings. Logic, reason and science are often dismissed in the minds of many people.

- Most if not all of us are filled with biases and prejudices that make us easy prey for a propagandist who knows how to "press our buttons". Adolf Hitler could always get a German crowd stirred up by the mention of the Versailles Treaty. One of the most important biases a human being has is to quickly accept statements that support his or her convictions.

- Propagandists can often get an audience to go along with them by telling the truth but not the whole truth. The United States Army tells young prospective recruits to "Be all you can be and join up" These young recruits are not told that two things they can be are dead and wounded.

- People are often more vulnerable to propaganda messages when they are mentally or physically tired. After a long day at work a person's critical thinking skills may lack their usual strength.

- A propagandist with charisma , a great voice, or a stunning appearance can stir up a crowd. Adolf Hitler really knew how to win over an audience with his bombastic speaking style filled with well practiced gestures accompanied with catch phrases.

- Many people are conformists. Once a propagandist gets a crowd roaring with enthusiasm, you can count on others initially less attracted to the propaganda message joining with the crowd in a show of support for what the speaker is saying.

- Self-centeredness and selfishness plus a great deal of greediness makes it easy for many people to swallow any propaganda message that appeals to these characteristics.

- The Pollyanna effect can be infectious and lead to an acceptance of a propaganda message. Some people have a foolishly or blindly optimistic view of people, events or visions of the future. Honest, God-fearing and moral folks who feel that all people are fundamentally good make a marvelous target for any unscrupulous propagandist.

- Most of us, at least sometimes, like to escape reality. Entertainment such as sports, motion pictures, radio, video games, television, day and night dreams and long walks in the park are just a few such escape practices. Often people like to hear utopian stories of the glory of a perfect world in which we all live prosperous and happy lives. Propagandists prey on people who feel that they deserve to live in fine homes, drive luxury cars and tour the world on luxurious vacations and send their children to the finest universities. Is it any wonder that politicians are notorious for making grandiose promises to the electorate?

- People who lack curiosity and are a bit lazy when it comes to thinking and analyzing messages fall prey to propagandists.

- People with submissive personality traits tend to yield to authority delight propagandists. An absence of any alternative points of view, usually due to censorship, makes acceptance of propaganda messages easier. This is why dictatorial governments rely on censorship to manipulate public opinion in their nations.

- It's generally easy to remember something that is repeated often. People remember slogans and phrases with greater ease than they remember entire speeches. President Franklin D. Roosevelt's statement that "The only thing we have to fear is fear itself" has been often repeated and is easily remembered. Who remembers the rest of his speech? Propagandists like to come up with slogans and sayings and repeat them often so that you'll not forget them.

Chapter 3

WHY IS PROPAGANDA VITAL AND NECESSARY?

Some selected reason for the vitality and necessity of propaganda:

- All humans live in a culture. Culture can be defined as a design for living and this world has thousands of designs. Even within a culture there are many sub-cultures, cultures that differ in some ways from the dominant culture. Sub-cultures have some different rules, beliefs, behaviors and values that set them apart. One characteristic shared by all cultures and sub- cultures is that they try to survive. The major way a culture is perpetuated is through the process of enculturation. Enculturation is the way in which young people are taught the basic beliefs, behaviors, values and customs of their respective cultures. One essential way to do this is to use many propaganda techniques to ensure that young people will grow up to keep their cultures alive and well. In a sense we are trapped by our cultures. We all at birth have no control over what political system we'll live under, what language we'll speak and, in most cases, what religion will be indoctrinating us. Life resembles a crap shoot!
- In America, and increasingly in the world, we see an enormous economic network. One term used to describe this economic phenomenon is globalization. One of the engines that drives an economy based on the purchasing power of consumers and the idea that the consumption of goods and services will grow indefinitely is advertising. Advertising is loaded with propaganda designed to

get consumers to spend their money. What might happen if there were no advertisements. We most likely would witness a massive economic depression.

- Ideologies need constant reinforcement to insure that their messages and goals can be achieved. Without a constant repetition of ideas, , rites, rituals, observances, use of signs and symbols, ideologies can weaken and even disappear. There are political, economic, religious and social ideologies of all kinds. Propaganda is a necessity to strengthen any ideology. In presidential campaigns in the United States millions of dollars are spent in appealing to the voters. Many religious groups advertise themselves on radio and television. The capitalist belief system is widely advertised in the mass media by corporate America.

- Most people live in a world in which suffering and death are all too common. Humans universally seem to desire comfort, security and hope. Often people want to believe that their lives can be made better. Because knowledge is finite while ignorance is infinite we are often forced to sidestep reason and logic in making choices to turn to faith. Propaganda can easily be used to fashion messages to the faithful. Without propaganda many people would lose the joy, comfort, hope and solace they desperately long for. Propaganda also helps people con themselves into a commitment to a faith in either a religion or ideology of some sort.

- Propaganda is an aid to groups trying to maintain the status quo (things as they are) as well as to groups that want to change the status quo. Any person or group seeking power will rely heavily on propaganda.

- War and propaganda go hand in hand. People need to be convinced that what their nation is doing is right, just and necessary. People need to be made to feel that any reluctance to support their nation in its conflicts is unpatriotic and close to being a treasonable action. In war propaganda the enemy is usually portrayed as being evil, monstrous, barbaric and uncivilized. All nations at war desperately need their people to support their troops. For this purpose propaganda is essential. Propaganda is also put to work to try to demoralize the enemy.

- Propaganda can be useful in educating people. This can be seen in messages of things to do and things not to do. We are cautioned not to smoke cigarettes to save us from possible lung cancer. We are also told not to take illegal drugs, not to eat fatty foods, not to drink and drive. In sexual matters we are told to just say no. In messages we hear what to do in an earthquake, what rules to follow in a big fire, how to make our homes safer and that we shouldn't go to the beach to see a tsunami wave.
- Propaganda seems to be a vital element in the "mating game". Men use any number of "lines" in order to get the attention of a prospective mate. Women try to make themselves attractive in a variety of ways. Many animals use a great many persuasive ways to win over a mate for propaganda is not an exclusively human activity when it comes to mating.

Propaganda is used to relieve people experiencing fear and stress. When the Soviet Union began the space age in 1957 many Americans worried that we were about to lose our supremacy in science and technology. People worried about the ability of our military to provide a high level of security for the nation. When President Kennedy presented his plan for America to send astronauts to the moon it lifted the spirits of millions of nervous Americans.

CHAPTER 4

HOW CAN WE GUARD AGAINST PROPAGANDA BASED ON FALSE INFORMATION OR AN EXTREMELY ONE-SIDED VIEW?

- We all need to protect ourselves against bad propaganda. I have selected a few ways I rely on to protect myself from unscrupulous propagandists.
- In any propaganda message, try to identify the techniques being used by the messenger.
- In any propaganda message, list the arguments being used by the messenger, then later on try to think of counter arguments.
- Think of taking a course in critical thinking or at least purchase a book on the subject. I did both and it really helped me.
- Try to check the accuracy of the information being delivered by a speaker or a writer.
- When possible, make an investigation of issues in your local community. For instance, visit schools, ask questions of the teachers and administrators and custodians. Talk to police and fire personnel, politicians, gardeners, etc.
- Record and replay a spoken propaganda message in order to seek out fallacies in the message.
- Try to track down the sources of the information being delivered.
- Investigate the background and credentials of the propagandist. Access to a computer should make this an easy task.

- Try to determine the agenda, the goals and the spin direction of the messenger.
- It is said that hope is the antidote for fear, but I feel that faith of any kind is often not accompanied by compelling evidence in support of it. Try not to be carried away by faith alone. Faith can be the dart that pierces the armor of an otherwise critical thinker.
- Adopt a skeptical attitude toward all mass media messages. Being skeptical will induce you to search for evidence that will either support or refute a statement.
- Watch television and listen to radio programs from foreign nations such as the BBC of the United Kingdom, Chinese international news and internet reports. Try reading foreign newspapers and news magazines. I like the *Economist* published in the United Kingdom. Don't live in an information bubble.
- Develop the trait of curiosity. Curious people make good researchers and tend to accumulate much information.
- Remind yourself that extraordinary claims require extraordinary and compelling evidence. If something seems too good to be true it probably isn't.
- Questions are often more important that answers so my friends who are scientists tell me. When you are at a town meeting, a lecture, a face to face conversation, a telephone call to a talk show program or just contemplating issues in your own mind, ask yourself questions.
- Don't make snap judgments. Give yourself time to think critically about an issue.
- Separate fact from opinion and inference. Thomas Jefferson tried to do this in his *Jefferson's Bible*.
- Study the body language of a speaker on television or at a public address or at a lecture. Body language is a growing research area for psychologists and there are books on the subject.
- Play close attention to the details of the propaganda message. Propagandists often try to sneak in their agenda items surrounded by true and reasonable statements, facts supported by logic and sound arguments. Don't let propagandists put one over on you.

I've always believed that two heads are better than one. If a propaganda's message is important to you, talk about the message with friends and others. Conversation with others can help a person to analyze and evaluate a propaganda message.

Chapter 5

WHO ARE SOME FAMOUS PERSUADERS IN WORLD HISTORY ?

We are all persuaders but, as in other comparisons some persuaders have a greater impact on human affairs than others. To list all important persuaders in history would be all but impossible. I've read about ancient, medieval and modern history. Fortunately the reader will be able to come up with many more names than in this list.

Ancient History

ALEXANDER THE GREAT (356-323 B.C.E.)
He was king of Macedonia. He conquered the Persian empire from the Mediterranean to India. He persuaded the people he conquered to accept Greek ideas and customs.

AMENHOTEP IV (Akhenatoon) (Dynasty 18 1353-1336 B.C.E.)
The traditional pantheon was abandoned for the worship of the sun and its life giving light. Worship of other gods was officially forbidden. The names of the traditional gods were chiseled from temples and monuments. His religion was abandoned upon his death.

ARISTOTLE (384-322 B.C.E.)

A Greek philosopher, educator, and scientist, student of Plato. Aristotle attended Plato's school in Athens known as the Academy. Aristotle was the teacher of Alexander the great. He founded a school in Athens called the Lyceum. His influence was almost lost but Arab and Sephardic scholars brought his work to European scholars who were greatly influenced by his ideas. Aristotle was given great respect by the Roman Catholic Church.

ASOKA (ASHOKA) (?-232 B.C.E.)

He ruled the Marian empire this includes modern day Afghanistan, Pakistan and India. He spread Buddhist ideas throughout his kingdom and sent Buddhist missionaries as far west as Greece.

BOUDICCA (? C.E. – 62 CE?)

Queen of the Iceni a tribe of Britons. She lived near present day Norfolk county, England. She led her tribe in a revolt against the Romans. The rebellion spread throughout East Anglia. She eventually was defeated, but became a lasting figure of heroism in England.

BUDDHA (563 B.C.E. – 483 B.C.E?)

Siddhartha Gautama was the founder of Buddhism. Buddha means "Enlightened one". He taught people to free themselves from all desire and worldly things to achieve complete happiness and peace and overcome suffering. Buddhism today numbers its followers in the hundreds of millions.

CATO THE ELDER (234 B.C.E. – 149 B.C.E.)

As a Roman censor and a high administrative official, he is said to have ended every speech with the words "Carthago delenda est! (Carthage must be destroyed!) His warnings encouraged the Romans to continue hostilities against Carthage which they destroyed in 146 B.C.E.

JULIUS CAESER (100 B.C.E? – 44 B.C.E)

He was Rome's greatest military leader. In his wars with German tribes in Gaul (Modern France) he prevented raids on Gaul by tribes on the eastern side of the Rhine by building a bridge across the Rhine showing the raiding tribes that they could not hide from retaliation. He also persuaded the Romans that he was a brilliant strategist.

CLEOPATRA (69 B.C.E. – 30 B.C.E.)
She persuaded Julius Caesar to put her on the throne of Egypt after her usurper had died.

CONFUCIUS (551 B.C.E? – 479 B.C.E?)
The most influential philosopher Confucianism became the official state philosophy for many centuries in China. Many of his ideas appear in the Analects.

CONSTANTINE THE GREAT (275 C.E? – 337 C.E?)
Under his rule Christianity became a legal religion in the Roman empire. Christianity went onto become the main faith in both the Western and Eastern Roman empires.

CYRUS THE GREAT (? – 530 B.C.E.)
Cyrus was the founder of the Persian empire. He persuaded many of the people he conquered to accept Persian rule by his policy of respecting local customs and religions.

HAMMURABI (1795 B.C.E. – 1750 B.C.E.)
He was the first king of the Babylonian empire, his empire controlled all of Mesopotamia. He is best known for the Code of Hammurabi. These laws were written on a large stone at a public place where all the locals could see it. By modern standards punishments were severe and were based on an eye for an eye justice.

HIPPOCRATES (460 B.C.E? – 380 B.C.E?)
This Greek physician is often called the father of medicine. The Hippocratic oath is still used in many medical schools throughout the world.

JESUS CHRIST (7-2 B.C.E? – 26-36 C.E?)
He used parables, brief stories, to get his views across to the people. Love and forgiveness for sinners who repent was one of his principles. He was

a champion of the poor and forgotten, calling for his followers to feed the hungry and clothe the naked. There are around 2 billion followers of Jesus globally today.

MENCIUS (390 B.C.E? – 305 B.C.E?)

He was one of the most influential thinkers in the development of Confucianism. He believed that human nature is basically good. He felt that if people are bad, it indicates that something is wrong with the organization of society. He also believed that people had the right to revolt against bad leaders. He defined a bad ruler as one who ignored the people's welfare and governed them unkindly.

MOSES (B.C.E?)

He led the Jews out of Egypt toward Canaan, the promised land. Moses was a political organizer, a military chief, a diplomat, a law maker, a judge and a religious leader. He persuaded many of his followers to accept the Ten Commandments.

MO TI /Mo Tzu (470 B.C.E. – 391 B.C.E.)

A Chinese philosopher whose doctrine of universal love challenged Confucianism for a considerable time during China's history. He challenged the Confucian concept of parental authority. He was a utopian thinker and was interested in logical systems rarely used in Chinese philosophy. When the first emperor of China started burning books and burying scholars alive, many of Mo's books were lost. These acts ended the influence of Mo Ti.

SAINT PAUL (5 – 67 C>E>

He was the most notable Christian missionary. He converted many people in the Mediterranean world to the new faith. His most important act of persuasion was to convince the Christian leadership that Christianity should accept all people into the faith not just Jews.

PLATO (424-423 B.C.E. – 348-347 B.C.E.)

He was a classical Greek philosopher. His mentor was Socrates and his most famous student was Aristotle. Plato helped to lay the foundations of western philosophy. He established a school of philosophy called the

Academy. Probably his best known work is *The Republic*. It deals with political theory and philosophy.

RAMSES II
He reigned from 1304 B.C.E. – 1237 B.C.E. He was the third ruler of the 19th Dynasty. He was a monument builder of notable structures such as the temple at Abydos, a finery temple known as the Ramesseum, at Thebes and the great Rock Temple at Abu Simbel in Nubian. He persuaded his people to be in awe of him and his monument still influences us today when thinking of him as a truly great leader.

SHI HUANG TI (259 B.C.E.?-210 B.C.E.)
He was a Chinese emperor who founded the Qin dynasty (221-206 B.C.E.). He, as the first emperor of China, created the first unified Chinese empire and added much to the Great Wall of china, created the first unified Chinese empire and added much to the Great wall of China. He standardized weights and measurement laws and the Chinese script. He is famous for burning writings and punishing scholars. To maintain his rule he used terror and severe punishments in persuading his people to submit to his rule.

SOCRATES (c470-399 B.C.E.)
A Greek philosopher and teacher. He is one of the most influential thinkers in Greek and Western history. He is known for his Socratic Method which features asking a person a series of questions designed to make the person think more clearly about his or her beliefs. He was accused of corrupting the youth of Athens with his questioning of the moral behavior of many prominent Athenians. He was condemned to death and swallowed poison in the form of hemlock even though he had a chance to escape. He demonstrated his commitment to moral behavior.

THEMOSTOCLES (c524-459 B.C.E.)
He was an Athenian soldier and statesmen. He advocated a policy of naval expansion in Athens to fight an expected Persian invasion of Greece. He argued persuasively that a recent discovery of a rich vein of silver should be used to build ships in defense of Athens. Many important

Athenians wanted the silver to be distributed amongst the elite members of Athenian society but Themostocles using misinformation was able to convince them to build the Athenian fleet.

ZOROASTER (628-551 B.C.E.)
He was a Persian religious leader and philosopher. Zoroaster was the founder of Zoroastrianism. This religion was thought to have been influential in the development of Judaism, Christianity, and Islam as one of the first monotheistic religions it emphasized that good and evil are separate entities at war with each other in the form of the god of good versus the god of evil. Both gods were said to have descended from the wise lord, Ahura Mazda.

MEDIEVAL HISTORY

PETER ABELARD (1079 – 1142 c>e>)
He was a French philosopher and theologian who helped develop what became the University of Paris. He urged the use of logic to understand and defend Christianity. He influenced the philosophical system called scholasticism.

ROGER BACON (1214 ? – 1294? C>e>)
He was an English philosopher and scientist who was one of the founders of experimental science. He used the inductive method in his scientific activities. His work influenced many scientists throughout Europe.

CHARLEMAGNE (9742 – 814 C.E.)
The most famous ruler of the Middle Ages , he conquered much of Western Europe. He revived the cultural life of the lands he ruled and forced the Saxons to accept Christianity. Charlemagne developed the feudal system in which lords got land in return for military service to the king.

ELEANOR OF AQUITAINE (1122 – 1204 c>e>)
She was the Duchess of Aquitaine and persuaded her people to embark on crusades to oust Moslems from their control of the holy lands of

the Near East. As a powerful independent woman she was involved in many political activities.

CHRISTOPHER COLUMBUS (1451 – 1506 C.E>)

An Italian navigator, his idea was to sail west to reach the riches of the East Indies. Columbus spent years trying to persuade Portugal, Spain and France of the worthiness of his mission. Spain's victory over Moslem Grenada led an official at the Spanish court to support him because there was now some funds available for an exploratory venture to the East Indies and a prospect of new wealth for Spain.

TIMUJIN (GENGHIS KHAN) (1162 ? – 1227 C>E>)

This Mongol conqueror founded the largest contiguous land empire in history. He was a military and political genius who united Mongolian and other nomadic tribes into a disciplined and effective fighting force. He created the first Mongol code of laws and promoted trade between China and Europe.

JUSTINIAN I (483 – 565 C.E.)

The greatest emperor of the Eastern Roman Empire, his wife Theodora was very influential in shaping Justinian's thoughts and actions. He established the Justinian Code

MUHAMMED (570 – 632 C.E.)

He is the central human figure of the religion of Islam. He is considered by Muslims to be God's messenger. This great Arab religious and military leader was born in Mecca in what is now Saudi Arabia. Mecca is the premier holy city of this faith. Islam has over one billion followers and is one of the world's fastest growing religions.

ST. THOMAS AQUINAS (1225 – 1274 C.E.)

The philosophy of Aquinas influenced theologians and scholars throughout Christian Europe. He is a most respected philosopher in the Roman Catholic Church. In his work Summa Theologica he systematically tried to explain Christian theology. He incorporated much of Aristotle's philosophy into Christian thought.

SAVONAROILA (1452 – 1498 C.E.)

Savonarola Girolano was a Dominican friar who became a fiery religious reformer in renaissance Italy. He tried to bring his reforms to the city of Florence and persuaded many to follow his precepts. He was excommunicated from the church for his attacks on the pope in Rome. The civil authorities in Florence hanged him. Lately the Roman Catholic Church is taking steps to elevate his image.

URBAN II (1042 – 1099 C.E.)

On November 27, 1095 Urban solemnly proclaimed the First Crusade against the infidels. He persuasively mobilized European chivalric elements to his cause. In 1099 the crusaders entered Jerusalem.

MODERN HISTORY

JOHN QUINCY ADAMS (1767 – 1848)

He helped develop the Monroe Doctrine to keep European powers out of the Western Hemisphere. Adams worked on the Treaty of Ghent which ended the War of 1812. As minister to Great Britain, he worked to keep the Canadian and United States border open and demilitarized.

SUSAN B. ANTHONY (1820 – 1906)

She was one of the first fighters for women's rights. She helped organize the world's first women's suffrage movement to give women the right to vote, to have equal education and property rights.

KEMAL ATATURK (1881 – 1938)

He was a Turkish army officer, revolutionary statesman and the founder of the Republic of Turkey. Ataturk became the first president of the Republic. His goal was to transform Turkey into a modern, democratic and secular state. Under his rule, women were given freedoms unheard of before. There was language reform that replaced Arabic script with a Latin script. Turkish artists were freed from Islamic restrictions.

SIMON BOLIVAR (1783 – 1830)

He was a great South American general who fought to liberate Venezuela from Spanish rule. He achieved independence for Bolivia, Colombia , Ecuador and his home territory of Venezuela. He persuaded many to follow him in his battles for independence but, contrary to his wishes, he was not able to permanently unite the areas he helped to liberate.

NAPOLEON BONAPARTE (1768 – 1821)

Napoleon was a great French general and political leader with a vision of unifying Europe under French rule. When he crowned himself emperor it seemed as though he was trying to recreate the old Roman Empire. He was a very persuasive commander who could easily get the support of his troops in his wars of conquest.

JOHN BROWN (1800 – 1859)

He was a radical abolitionist who attempted to free the slaves. Some say that he indirectly helped bring about the American Civil War. He wanted to keep Kansas from being a slave state. John Brown persuaded family members and others to stage a raid on Harper's Ferry. His group was either killed or captured by a mixed force including U.S. Marines led by Robert E. Lee. John Brown was eventually captured by federal forces and was hanged.

JOHN CALVIN (1509 – 1564)

One of the chief leaders of the Protestant Reformation, he is known for his concept of predestination. His idea is that your fate after death has already been determined. If you are successful in this life it is likely that you will have been one of those chosen to receive entry into heaven. Puritans, Huguenots , Presbyterians and other Protestant groups were influenced by his theological ideas.

FIDEL CASTRO (1926 - ?)

A leader of Cuba from 1959 until the reigns of power were transferred to his brother, he overthrew the Batista dictatorship and seized American owned properties. His acceptance of a communist system as well as ties to the Soviet Union saured relationships between Cuba and the United States. This situation was highlighted by the Cuban Missile Crisis.

CHRISTINA OF SWEDEN (1626 – 1689)

She was Queen regnant of Sweden from 1632 to 1689. She persuaded her people to be tolerant of others. She set a good example by being kind to Jews and followers of other faiths.

CHIEF JOSEPH (1849 – 1904)

Joseph was the chief of the Wallowa band of the Nez Perce. When General Oliver O'Howard attempted to forcibly remove his band and other "non-treaty" Native Americans to a reservation in Idaho, Joseph advocated peaceful relations with whites. His view did not help his people who fled for freedom in Canada. After a prolonged battle with the U.S. Cavalry, the Nez Perce surrendered. In an attempt to get fair treatment, for his people, he went to Washington D.C. and pled his case before President Rutherford B. Hayes. The president helped Joseph and his band to their general home territory.

SIR WINSTON CHURCHILL (1874 – 1965)

He was the prime minister of the United Kingdom during World War II. His courage, his way with words and his faith in a final victory over the Axis powers inspired the British to fight their enemies with renewed vigor.

NICOLAUS COPERNICUS (1473 – 1543)

He was a Polish astronomer who developed the theory that Earth is a moving planet that revolves around the sun. His ideas helped to persuade scientists like Galileo in Italy and Kepler in Germany to perform experiments with results that supported the Copernican theory.

CHARLES DARWIN (1809 – 1882)

He was an English naturalist who realized and demonstrated that all species of life have evolved over time from common ancestors through the process of natural selection. His book *On the Origin of Species* (1859) laid much of the foundation of modern biology.

DENIS DIDEROT (1713 – 1784)

He was a French philosopher and writer famous for his encyclopedia. Diderot was a noted figure in the Enlightenment . His articles included many topics of great influence on intellectuals throughout Europe.

BENJAMIN DISRAELI (1804 – 1881)
Disraeli was an English statesman who helped create the modern Conservative party. He arranged for Queen Victoria to get the title Empress of India. He worked to contain the growing power of Russia.

DOROTHEA DIX (1802 – 1887)
Dix was a 19th century activist on behalf of the indigent masses present in American society. Through a vigorous program of lobbying state legislators and the United States Congress, she helped to create the first generation of American mental asylums as they were then called. She was instrumental in the founding of the first public mental hospital in Pennsylvania.

FREDERICK DOUGLASS (1817 – 1895)
Douglass was an abolitionist, educator and writer who fought against slavery and for women's rights. He was the first African American citizen to be appointed to a high office in the United States. Douglass lectured extensively in America and the United Kingdom.

MARY BAKER EDDY (1821 – 1010)
Eddy was an American religious leader. She founded the Church of Christ, Scientist in 1879. She taught that spiritual healing without modern medical intervention could succeed in healing her followers. *Science and Health with Key to the Scriptures* published in 1875, is the textbook for Christian Scientists. She founded the daily newspaper, the Christian Science Monitor in 1908. This daily as of late is switching from paper to the internet.

ALBERT EINSTEIN (1879 – 1955)
In 1939, at the urging and with the help of the Hungarian physicist Leo Szilard, Einstein wrote a letter to President Franklin D. Roosevelt. The letter said that the German scientists might be working on an atomic bomb. The letter, with Einstein's signature, led to the establishment of the Manhattan Project and resulted in the making of the first atomic bomb in 1945.

DWIGHT D. EISENHOWER (1890 – 1969)

In his farewell address to the nation he gave a warning to the American people when he said "We must guard against acquisition of unwarranted influence, whether sought or unsought, by the "military industrial complex". His words are still in the minds of many today.

QUEEN ELIZABETH (1533 – 1603)

Elizabeth, as Queen of England, made the Church of England the premier Christian denomination in the nation. Her policies helped to make England a prosperous country and gained her the respect of her people. She worked to strengthen the naval power of England.

HENRY FORD (1863 – 1947)

Ford was the leading maker of American automobiles in the early 1900's. He worked to make an affordable car for average people. Early cars were expensive and were made for wealthy people. In 1924 his car sold for $290. In 1914 Ford raised the minimum wage of his workers to $5.00 a day. He reduced the work day from 9 to 8 hours a day. He greatly influenced others in the automobile industry to adopt many of his ideas.

BENJAMIN FRANKLIN (1706 – 1790)

Franklin was an American statesman and scientist who was a major contributor to the structure of the American government. He persuaded the French to support the cause of the American Revolution.

GALILEO (1564 – 1642)

This Italian astronomer, naturalist and physicist has been called the father of modern experimental science. He supported the Copernican view of a sun centered solar system. His greatest contribution was in stimulating and inspiring others to pursue experimental science.

MOHANDAS GHANDI (1869 – 1948)

Gandhi was a great political and spiritual leader in the 1900's. He helped free India from British control through the use of non-violent protests. In the salt march of 1930 , Gandhi and his followers marched 240 miles to the sea to make salt from the sea water to protest the Salt Act which made it illegal to make salt not bought in government stores.

WILLIAM LLOYD GARRISON (1895 – 1879)
Garrison attacked slavery in the 1830's. In 1831 he published *The Liberator* which was full of anti-slavery articles. He also argued for women's rights. His activities gained him much support as well as much opposition.

BILL GATES (1955 - ☺)
Gates is the co-founder of the Microsoft Corporation. He founded the Bill and Melinda Gates Foundation. This foundation supports many charitable causes and highlights many of the world's great needs. Gates designed programs for computers. His work helped to bring the computer into the homes of average people.

JOSEPH GOEBBELS (1897 – 1945)
Goebbels was the official propagandist of Nazi Germany. He lent support to the major goals of the Nazi government under Adolf Hitler. Some of these goals were invading other nations to acquire more living space for Germany, the extermination of Jews and others and a commitment to victory through total war.

ALEXANDER HAMILTON (1755? – 1804)
Hamilton was the first United States Secretary of the Treasury. One of his policies was for the federal government to assume state debts incurred during the Revolutionary War. Hamilton persuaded both Thomas Jefferson and James Madison to lend him their support. The bill assuming state debts narrowly passed the House of Representatives in 1790. Hamilton is credited with putting the nation's financial system in a good condition.

WILLIAM RANDOLF HEARST (1863 – 1951)
Hearst was an American newspaper magnate. In his papers he lent support to the cause of the Cuban people against the rule of the Spanish. Some people accused Heart of helping bring America into conflict with Spain. He used sensational drawings in his papers to influence public opinion.

HENRY VIII (1491 – 1547)

He was the king of England and was the second monarch of the House of Tudor. Henry separated the Anglican church from the Roman hierarchy and became the supreme head of the Church of England. His actions helped to erode the power of the Vatican.

THEODORE HERZL (1860 – 1904)

Herzl was an Austrian Jewish journalist who founded modern political Zionism. He was greatly influenced by the Dreyfus case. Dreyfus was a French Jewish officer in the French army who was falsely charged. Some people at the trial screamed "Death to the Jews". Herzl's most persuasive message was that the Jewish people deserved to be able to live in a Jewish state located in their ancient homeland.

ADOLF HITLER (1889 – 1945)

Hitler led the Nazi party and became the chancellor of Germany in 1933. He soon became dictator in Germany until his suicide in 1945. Hitler was a great persuader using his charismatic speaking skills backed by a huge propaganda machine. In all probability, few of his supporters realized that their beloved Fuhrer was going to be their undertaker and leave German cities in ruins.

HO CHI MINH (1890 – 1969)

He was a communist revolutionary leader of Vietnam. He fought tirelessly to free Vietnam from French rule, then he took on the Japanese invaders and when Japan lost the war he fought the returning French. After the French left he took on the invading Americans. Vietnam emerged from fighting America as a victorious nation. Ho Chi Minh had inspired many of his people to fight for independence.

RON HUBBARD (1911 – 1986)

Ron Hubbard established the philosophy called scientology. He wrote *Dianetics, the Modern Science of Mental Health* in 1950. Scientology is now a growing movement which has as one of its chief goals spiritual freedom.

ANDREW JACKSON (1767 – 1845)

Jackson was President of the United States from 1829 to 1837. He opposed the Bank of the United States, the nullification idea of Calhoun in which a state could ignore any federal law not being in a state's interest and the right of the Cherokees to keep their land in Georgia. In all these matters he demonstrated his great powers of persuasion.

THOMAS JEFFERSON (1743 – 1826)

Jefferson was the third President of the United States. His persuasiveness was witnessed by his actions. In his Declaration of Independence he used many arguments to support his case before Americans and the world. He faced opposition to his Louisiana Purchase and won acceptance of his action which involved questions of legality. He saw America expanding westward and had Lewis and Clark go on an exploratory expedition. He used persuasion to convince people that the separation of church and state was a good policy.

BENITO JUAREZ (1806 – 1872)

Juarez was one of Mexico's greatest political leaders. He led his country's struggle to free itself from French control. This Zapotec Indian was elected President of Mexico in 1861. He wanted the separation of church and state and was greatly influenced by political leaders in the United States. President Lincoln and General Grant assisted him in his battles against French forces. Juarez inspired his people to fight for their freedom.

JOHN FITZGERALD KENNEDY (1917 – 1963)

He was the first President of the United States who was of the Roman Catholic faith. He was persuasive in many ways. He sold the idea of a voyage through space to the moon, he got support from young Americans for his Peace Corps initiative and he persuaded the Russians to remove their missiles from Cuba.

W. K. KELLOGG (1860 – 1951)

Kellogg experimented with a new breakfast food called "corn flakes". In 1906 Kellogg organized a cereal company and with a skillful use of advertising his company grew large and successfully. Many people all over the world eat his flakes for breakfast today.

MARTIN LUTHER KING (1929 – 1968)

This African-American civil rights leader is known for his policy of non-violence. He was greatly influenced by Gandhi's resistance to British rule in India. When there was a march to Washington D.C. in 1963, King delivered his "I Have a Dream" speech". This was one of the greatest speeches in American history and his words inspired millions to support the civil rights movement.

V. I. LENIN (1870 – 1924)

Lenin founded the Communist Party in Russia and established the world's first Communist Party dictatorship. He wrote many works that were distributed among radical revolutionaries. He especially wrote many articles for *Pravda* (The Truth), a revolutionary newspaper. Lenin was a powerful orator and persuaded many people to follow his leadership.

ABRAHAM LINCOLN (1809 – 1865)

Lincoln was the sixteenth President of the United States. He tried to persuade the people of the United States to maintain the Union by stressing the point that "a house divided cannot stand". His Emancipation Proclamation was a great first step in the eventual abolition of slavery in the 13th Amendment to the Constitution. He advocated a policy of lenience to the southern states returning to the Union but his assassination put this policy on hold.

MACHIAVELLI (1469 – 1527)

Machiavelli was an Italian statesman and writer who is often credited with being the father of political science. His best known work is *The Prince* published in 1532. He explained politics realistically.

JAMES MADISON (1751 – 1836)

Madison was the fourth President of the United States. He played a role in the creation of the system of checks and balances among the three branches of government : the executive, legislative and judicial, Madison argued for the separation of church and state and drafted the first ten amendments to the Constitution – the Bill of Rights.

MARIA THERESA (1717 – 1780)
She was the archduchess of Austria, holy Roman Empress and Queen of Hungary and Bohemia. She saved the Hapsburg lads from dismemberment and persuaded many to accept reforms of various kinds.

COTTON MATHER (1663 – 1728)
Cotton Mather was a leading Puritan minister and theologian in colonial New England. He was praised for supporting inoculations against smallpox during a 1721 epidemic in Boston. Some accused him of lending support to witch hunts in Salem, Massachusetts.

HORACE MANN (1796 – 1859)
He played a leading role in establishing state-supported and state-funded mandatory attendance school systems in the United States. In 1839 Mann helped found the nation's first state-supported normal school (teacher training school).

KARL MARX (1818 – 1883)
Marx was one of the most influential thinkers of the 19th century. His writings formed the foundation of political and economic communism. He predicted the fall of capitalism but didn't realize the effects of unionism in giving benefits to workers. In 1848 Marx and Engels wrote the Communist Manifesto. Marx's most ambitious work was *Das Kapital*, (Capital). Fear of communism may have caused nations with capitalistic economic systems to make reforms in order to fend off communist influences.

LUCRETIA MOTT (1793 – 1880)
Mott was a Quaker minister, abolitionist, social reformer and proponent of women's rights. She delivered sermons on her anti-slavery views and preached at Black parishes. She was ahead of her time as women had to wait until 1920 in order to vote in federal elections.

JOHN MUIR (1838 – 1914)
Muir was an explorer, naturalist and writer who campaigned for the conservation of water and forests in the United States. He influenced the Congress of the United States to pass the Yosemite National Park Bill in 1890. He helped to persuade president Theodore Roosevelt to set aside 148 million acres of forest reserves.

BENITO MUSSOLINI (1883 – 1945)
Mussolini was one of the founders of Italian fascism. He became the dictator of Italy and won admiration for his public works programs, improvement in job opportunities, progress in transportation infrastructure and his making peace with the Vatican. He used propaganda to persuade the people of Italy that he was a great leader. A popular slogan under his rule was "Mussolini ha sempre ragione", (Mussolini is always right).

CARY NATION (1846 – 1911)
Cary Nation was a leader of the temperance movement which opposed the sale and consumption of alcohol in pre-prohibition America. She would often enter an establishment that served alcoholic drinks and throw stones at liquor bottles and then use her hatchet to makeup the bar. She claimed that she had an experience of receiving a message from God and she increased her acts of vandalism. Several saloons posted notices by their doors saying "All nations welcome except Cary". The Women's Christian Temperance Union dedicated a memorial to her at her grave site.

JAWAHARLAL NEHRU (1869 – 1964)
Nehru was the first prime minister of India. He studied science at Trinity College, Cambridge University in the United Kingdom. As prime minister he persuaded India's government to develop the nation's educational system. He is praised for creating world class educational institutions of medicine, technology and management. India's rise as a scientific and technological power owes much to Nehru's efforts.

KWAME NKRUMA (1909 – 1972)
Nkruma was a leader of Ghana, a nation in West Africa. He was a persuasive force in Pan-Africanism. This was the idea that African nations should unite. In 1963 he wrote the book *Africa Must Unite*.

THOMAS PAINE (1737 – 1809)
Paine was an English pamphleteer who emmigrated to colonial America. His influential and widely read pamphlet *Common Sense,* written in 1776, argued forcibly for the American colonies to strive for independence from Great Britain.

LOUIS PASTEUR (1822 – 1895)
Pasteur was a French scientist who discovered that diseases are spread by bacteria. He also found that living things come from living things and that there were ways to stop the spread of bacterial diseases. He persuaded people in the field of public health to adopt his measures such as using heat to kill bacteria, pasteurization, and vaccinating people against serious diseases.

COMMADOR PERRY (1794 – 1858)
Commodore Perry was a United States naval officer best known for the opening of Japan to Western trade and diplomacy. His demonstration of advanced military weapons as well as other technologies such as a railway led the leadership of Japan to realize that modernization was necessary to prevent Western nations from colonizing their nation.

PETER THE GREAT (1672 – 1725)
Peter was the Russian czar who transformed Russia from an isolated agricultural society into a empire on a par with European powers. In his reign he established his capital at St. Petersburg , a gateway to Europe across the Baltic Sea. In order to Europeanize his people, he ordered that all men shave off their beards. He wanted Russia to copy the ways of European nations. Peter encouraged the development of industry and science in order to modernize the country.

FRANCISCO PIZARRO (1478 – 1541)
Pizarro was a Spanish conqueror of the Inca Empire. After his expedition to South America, he returned to Spain and persuaded King Charles I to appoint him governor in Peru. After Pizarro's forces captured the Inca ruler Atahualpa, he required vast amounts of treasure for his release. The Incas accepted his request but after the riches were delivered, the Spanish executed Atahualpa.

JAMES KNOX POLK (1795 – 1849)

Polk was the eleventh President of the United States. He pursued an expantionist policy in keeping with the philosophy of Manifest Destiny which held that it was the destiny of the United States to rule the land between the Atlantic and Pacific Oceans. He made a peaceful acquisition of the Oregon Territory claimed by Britain and gave up American claims to British Columbia. Polk wanted California and other Mexican territory in the West. He arranged to take this land by war. The Mexican-American War started in 1846 and ended in 1848. America now included California and other former Mexican lands. With the discovery of gold in California, Polk's policy of expansion seemed wise to many Americans.

ELEANOR ROOSEVELT (1884 – 1962)

Eleanor Roosevelt was First Lady of the United States from 1933 to 1945. She was a delegate to the United Nations General Assembly and played a part in drafting the Universal Declaration of Human Rights. She was vocal in her support of the African-American Civil Rights Movement. She was outspoken in her support of Marian Anderson in 1939 when the African-American singer was denied the use of Washington's Constitution Hall and was instrumental in the subsequent concert being held on the steps of the Lincoln Memorial. She was a great persuader in the cause of tolerance for Americans regardless of race, gender or ethnicity.

FRANKLIN D. ROOSEVELT (1882 – 1945)

He was the President of the United States from 1933 to 1945. FDR, as he was often called , is the only president to have served four terms. He began his presidency during the Great Depression of the 1930s. Roosevelt created the New Deal, a series of policies designed to restore the nation's economic health. As soon as he took office, he tried to overcome opposition to his politics by reaching out to the American people with radio programs called "fireside chats". His persuasive appeals won the support of American voters who gave him victories at the ballot box.

THEODORE ROOSEVELT (1858 – 1919)
He was the twenty-sixth President of the United States. Teddy, as he was often called, was the first president to consider the long-term need for the efficient use of the nation's natural resources. He urged the Congress to establish the United States Forest Service. Teddy was very persuasive in asking the Congress to pass the Pure Food and Drug Act of 1906.

GEORGE SAND (1804 – 1876)
Sand was a French woman novelist and dramatist known for her strong feminist views. She wore men's clothing and displayed herself in public. Her most notable relationship was with the composer Frederick Chopin. It is thought that the good care she gave to him extended his life. She opposed the inequality of men and women and became a symbol for many women opposed to the gender status quo.

SHAKA ZULU (1787 – 1828)
Shaka was a great Zulu king and conqueror. He brought more than 100 chiefdoms together to make a strong Zulu kingdom in southern Africa. Shaka was able to persuade many of his enemies , after their defeat in battle, to join him. He imposed strict discipline on his soldiers and introduced many novel military innovations.

UPTON SINCLAIR (1878 – 1968)
Sinclair was an American writer and reformer. He became famous as a "muckraker", a writer who digs up the dirt on people, companies and governmental agencies that do a disservice to the nation and its citizens. His book, *The Jungle*, published in 1906, revealed terrible conditions in the meat packing industry. Sinclair's book lent support to the passing of the nation's first pure food laws.

ADAM SMITH (1723 – 1790)
Smith is considered by many to be the founder of modern economics. His major book was *The Wealth of Nations*, published in 1776. He argued that nations should encourage competition and that the marketplace should not be controlled so that free trade can flourish. His ideas are still influential today.

DR. SPOCK (1903 – 1999)

Dr. Spock was an American pediatrician. His book *Baby and Child Care*, published in 1946, was one of the best sellers of all time. His ideas on child care have influenced several generations of parents.

JOSEPH STALIN (1879 – 1953)

Stalin was the dictator of the Soviet Union from 1929 to 1953. He ruled by terror and eliminated all who opposed him. He transformed the Soviet Union from an underdeveloped agricultural country into an industrial and military power. This cruel leader had the blood of millions of his citizens on his hands. It could be said that his draconian measures and behavior played a role in the defeat of Nazi Germany.

ELIZABETH CADY STANTON (1815 – 1902)

Stanton was an early leader in the women's rights movement. She also was an abolitionist. In 1848 Stanton and Lucretia Mott called the nation's first women's rights convention held in Seneca Falls, New York. In 1878, Stanton persuaded Senator Aaron A. Sargent of California to sponsor a woman suffrage amendment to the Constitution of the United States. This proposal failed to pass but was reintroduced every year until 1919 when the Congress finally approved it as the 19th Amendment in 1920.

HARRIET BEECHER STOWE (1811 – 1896)

Stowe is best remembered for her novel *Uncle Tom's Cabin*, published in 1852 was the best selling novel of the 19th century. This book intensified the split between the North and the South and may have helped bring about the Civil War.

SUN YAT SEN (1866 – 1925)

He was a Chinese statesman and revolutionary leader who fought to create a Republic of China. The republic was established in 1912 and followed Sun's Three People's Principles, nationalism, democracy and socialism.

HARRIET TUBMAN (1920 – 1913)

Tubman was an African-American abolitionist, humanitarian and Union spy during the Civil War. After escaping from captivity, she made thirteen missions to rescue over seventy slaves using the network of anti-slavery activists and safe houses known as the Underground Railroad. In her postwar years she struggled for women's suffrage.

GEORGE WASHINGTON (1732 – 1799)

Washington was the first President of the United States under the Constitution. He was the commander of the Continental Army. Washington tried to persuade future politicians to stay out of foreign entanglements. He didn't favor political parties and their resultant partisanship. Washington only served two terms setting a pattern only broken once in the nation's history.. With the passage of the 25th Amendment, Washington's example became the law of the land.

CHAIM WEIZMANN (1874 – 1952)

Weitzman, a Zionist, was the first president of Israel. He was a key figure in the creation of Israel. British government leaders suggested that Uganda would make a possible place for Jewish settlement. Weizmann persuaded the influential British politician Lord Balfour that Jews would prefer to settle in their traditional homeland. As a scientist he wanted to develop higher education in Israel. He founded the Weizmann Institute of Science and lobbied to create the Hebrew University of Jerusalem.

WOVOKA (1856> - 1932)

Wovoka was a Paiute religious leader who founded the Ghost Dance religion in 1890. He claimed that God told him to tell his people to live peaceably and love others. His followers were told that they would not grow old or suffer illness or hunger if they did the Ghost Dance. If the dancing was well done the dead would return.

CHAPTER 6

WHAT IS THE EVOLUTIONARY HISTORY OF PERSUASION??

The history of persuasion could fill a good sized library, so I have selected a few examples of early persuasion from both animal and human history showing the persuasive behavior of many life forms.

In the Judeo-Christian tradition, there is a story from the book of Genesis that tells of the first persuader, a serpent, who convinced Eve, the first woman, to eat the forbidden fruit of the tree of good and evil. Many persuaders down to the present day have followed in the path of the snake.

Looking at life from a biological perspective, it seems that both humans and animals have been endowed with bodily features and patterns of behavior designed to persuade others. I feel that persuasion is a trans-species phenomenon.

One can recognize two powerful stimuli seen in animal evolution one being the need for defense against predators and two, being the need to mate and reproduce to avoid extinction. Since the beginning of life, nature's plan seems to have been that some animals will be predators while others will be prey. It's the hunters versus the hunted. It appears that there has always been an arms race in animal evolution between these two groups.

Persuasion as a factor in defense can be seen among many animals. The use of rattles by a rattle snake to ward off any would be predator is certainly of great benefit to the snake. The malodorous defense, used by a skunk, helps this animal to avoid becoming a predator's dinner. Baboons, elephants and chimpanzees often use group cooperation and action to defend themselves from predators.

In the case of early humans , who left the jungle for life in the relatively treeless savavvah, a female with one or more children would be easy prey. What could provide for their protection, nutrition and survival over the long term? I think that belonging to a band of related and cooperative individuals and making a bond with a male would be important. Being open to year around sexual relations would be a great help in the bonding process. All of these opinions are speculative because prehistory means that there are no written records of what actually was going on in human affairs.

Looking at mating matters, we see a powerful need for animals to be good persuaders to successfully mate. You can see a male peacock with an elaborate, colorful feathered fan designed to attract the attention of a female peacock. The male is trying to persuade the female to consider him to be a fit mate. This may be a case of hard wiring in the peacock's brain but it certainly is a persuasive act.

Trying to construct the behavior of early humans is a guessing game. It's my guess that some behaviors of present day chimpanzees might have been seen among early human groups.

Some male chimps try to demonstrate their power and strength by making aggressive displays. They swing through the trees shouting and screaming and sometimes carry sticks to strike out at bushes and trees to shower the air with leaves in all directions.

Humans became unique in the animal world when they developed the ability to speak and create languages. Nobody really knows exactly when our species first began to speak. It seems possible that some early hominids, perhaps 400,000 years ago or more , began to develop rudimentary speech. We're not absolutely sure that our close cousins, Homo Neanderthalensis could speak. What we do know is that the human trait of speech is one of the greatest adaptations to the need for complex organization in the history of our species. With speech we can do what no other animal can do. We can speak about events in the past, present and future. A group of humans hunting down animals would be handicapped without the ability to speak. I imagine that along with speech came the ability to sing, tell stories and develop a better sense of history and traditions in the form of oral history learned through repetition and memorization. Being able to persuade others was greatly enhanced by the gift of tongues.

Before the invention of writing systems, the most effective way to try to influence people was by the use of oratory. In ancient Greece and Rome, oratory was a highly developed skill among political and military leaders. One only has to read about orations delivered in the Roman Senate to be impressed by the rhetorical skills displayed by the notable members of that body.

A way to increase the reach of the human voice appeared in Europe in the 16th century C.E. - the megaphone. By using a megaphone, a speaker can channel his or her voice over a greater distance.

By far the most significant advance in carrying the human voice far, wide and fast was the invention of the telephone. The telephone brought voice communication over wires. The invention of this device is generally credited to Alexander Graham Bell who unveiled his invention in 1876. Phone use became widespread swiftly. In the late 19th and throughout the 20th century the growth of phone use steadily increased. With the introduction of cell phones, it looks like the 21st century will witness the dominance of wireless voice communication for cell phones give people mobility.

Not content with inventing the telephone, Alexander Graham Bell invented the loudspeaker. He patented the first electric loudspeaker as part of his telephone in 1876.

In 1876 Emile Berliner, inspired by Alexander Graham Bell's telephone, invented the first microphone used as a telephone voice transmitter.

Another great development was in recording sound. Thomas Alva Edison patented his phonograph in 1878. Sound recording has come in many forms from wax cylinders, to discs, to tapes and on to compact discs. The recording of sound replaced silent films. The human voice came into people's living rooms with the coming of the radio. In 1895, Guglielmo Marconi sent the first radio communication of Morse Code messages. Radio developed rapidly and the great age of the medium started about 1925 and ended about 1950. In America President Franklin Delano Roosevelt used his Fireside Chats , radio programs in the 1930's, to build support for his policies. A friend of mine was on a bicycle tour of Germany in 1938 and told me that the manager of the small hotel in which he was staying came to the lobby , dressed in a Nazi uniform, and saluted the radio when the Fuhrer's voice brought his ideas into German homes. Today, radio is still important. Talk show hosts are currently shapers of much public opinion.

Motion pictures entrance many people everywhere. Motion pictures began their development in the 19th century. In America, Edison developed motion pictures in the 1880's. As a propaganda tool, motion pictures are extremely effective. D. W. Griffith produced *Birth of a Nation* in 1915. This film portrayed stereotypical characters and expressed racist attitudes. Southern attitudes after the Civil War were given credibility and justification. In Nazi Germany Leni Riefenstahl produced *Triumph of the Will* (1934), a propaganda masterpiece that made Adolf Hitler a god-like bigger than life personality. Films will undoubtedly continue to be an important part of a propagandist's tool kit.

Painting, sculpture and architecture are three major art forms with fairly long histories in the human experience. Art and architecture have long been used in persuading people to submit to and honor gods, goddesses and elite political, religious and economic individuals and groups with power and authority.

Painting seems to have emerged in the stone age when hunter-gatherers painted scenes on cave walls of the animals they hunted. From 30,000 to 8,000 years ago, beautiful paintings were produced in places such as Lascaux in France and Altamira in Spain. Later on, Egyptian, Greek and Roman paintings had mainly religious themes. In Europe during the Middle Ages and Renaissance eras, paintings usually were of important individuals or religious subjects. In modern times many paintings deal with social problems, political ideology and war. Propagandists have used paintings to dramatize their causes. Commercial advertisers have found paintings to be useful in winning over consumers. In many art schools commercial art is a major subject.

Sculpture has been produced by humans ever since the age of Paleolithic hunter-gatherers. The Venus of Willendorf, a statuette of a woman with exaggerated obese characteristics, has been dated at about 24,000 to 22,000 B.C.E. The carved palette of King Narmer was made about 2,920 B.C.E. in Egypt. It commemorated the victory of Upper Egypt over Lower Egypt. This art piece is a great example of political propaganda. Greek and Roman sculpture glorified gods, goddesses and political and military notables. Religious subjects dominated the sculpture of the Middle Ages and Renaissance in Europe. One only has to see Michelangelo's statue of David , a character from the Bible, to see a great example of religious propaganda.

Looking at Asia, we see the great statue of Buddha at Kamakura, Japan. India is full of statues covering vast temple complexes. Buddha statues are found in great numbers in China, Japan and Southeast Asia. Judaism and Islam have rejected statues , probably to reinforce the prohibition against idol worship before the introduction of monotheism in the Near East. In the Pacific world we see the huge stone heads at Easter Island and in Meso America at places such as the Mayan city of Copan Honduras, we see large statues of Mayan kings.

In modern times, statues generally seem to feature political and military figures. The statues of Lenin, Stalin, Saddam Hussein , Kemal Ataturk and United States presidents on Mt. Rushmore, South Dakota and in

Washington D.C. are just a few examples of statues as propaganda tools for hero building.

Photography is a modern art form that does many things that used to be done by painters. Most family portraits today are photographed not painted. Photography has evolved into a medium with many branches. Museums worldwide display photographs as art pieces worthy of the same respect that in the past was usually reserved for traditional arts. Photography shows that a picture really can be worth a thousand words. The French inventor Joseph Nicephone Niepce made the world's first photograph in 1826 at Paris. In the 1830's developments continued to improve photography. Across the Atlantic in America, Mathew Brady broke new ground in war news photography. His photographs brought the Civil War into the homes of Americans thereby creating a revulsion against the horrors of the conflict. As time progressed photography entered the tool kit of propagandists. Think of the little Vietnamese girl running down a road screaming in agony from the effects of an American napalm bomb. This photograph turned many Americans against the war.

Given that our species has been on earth for an estimated 100,000 years or more, complex architecture is a fairly recent development. The following selected list of major structures is an attempt to show how buildings have been and are used as instruments of persuasion often used to advance the status of political, economic or religious groups as well as the status of cities and nations:

1. Megalithic (large stone) structures rise in Brittainy in France about 4,800 B.C.E. It is thought that these structures had some religious significance but we have no written records to go by.

2. A proto-ziggurat (a mound of bricks) is built at Uruk in Mesopotamia about 3,200 B.C.E. It is felt that ziggurats were religious structures and many of them were erected on the land between the Tigris and Euphrates Rivers.

3. The step pyramid of King Djoser at Seqqara, Egypt was built about 2,630 B.C.E. The architect was Imhotep, the first recorded architect in history. The six-tired pyramid was covered in white limestone and glorified the god-king.

4. The Great Pyramid of the Pharaoh Kufu was built at Giza, Egypt about 2,555 B.C.E. At 480 feet high it was the world's tallest building until Lincoln Cathedral was completed in 1,300 C.E.

5. The Ishtar Gate was built in Babylon, Iraq about 600 B.C.E. The gate was covered with blue glazed decorated bricks and the structure was involved in religious processions. King Nebuchadnezzar commissioned this gate to glorify his reign. The gate has been reconstructed in a museum in Berlin, Germany.

6. The Nergal Gate at Nineveh was one of 15 gates , each named after an Assyrian god, that was the chief entrance to the capital city of the Assyrian Empire. It was built about 700 B.C.E.

7. The Palace at Knossos, Crete was built about 1700 to 1400 B.C.E. The five story palace was a Minoan political center and a structure with many innovative features such as indoor baths, drainage to sewers , toilets with seats, etc.

8. The Parthenon is a Doric temple built on the Acropolis (high city) in Athens, Greece. It was built from 447 to 442 B.C.E. and was the spiritual center for the Athenians. The Greek architects knew that perfectly straight columns would not look right to the human eye so they made their columns bulge somewhat in the center so they look right.

9. The Colosseum was built in Rome from 72 to 80 C.E. The amphitheater, which was designed to seat 50,000 spectators, provided entertainment for the people of the city and gave emperors a chance to gain the favor of their subjects by staging elaborate spectacles. This structure became the model for our large stadiums today.

10. The Pantheon (temple for all the gods) was built in Rome about 125 C.E. Its dome sits on a cylindrical base and has an oculus (opening) at its top. The dome is built with nonreinforrced concrete..

11. The Palace of Darius was built at Persepolis, in modern Iran, from 518 to 486 B.C.E. Next to the palace was the Apodama, a large ceremonial hall, rising 82 feet high. Visitors to the Persian capital must have been impressed with the power and glory of Darius and his empire.

12. Hagia Sophia is a Byzantine church constructed in Constantinople, modern Istanbul, Turkey, from 532 to 537 C.E. It has a huge dome built on a square base which was a great innovation in the construction of domed buildings. Some historians think that this grand church played a part in the conversian of Russians to Christianity. Princess Olga of Kiev visited Constantinople and was most likely impressed by this great church,

13. The Great Stupa at Sanchi was built about 200 B.C.E. near Bopal in Madhya Pradesh state, India. A stupa is a brick and plaster hemisphere , usually containing a relic of the Buddha.

14. The Kofuku – ji Temple pagoda is a Buddhist shrine. It is in Nara, Japan and was reassembled about 600 C.E. This pagoda is one of the oldest wooden buildings in the world. A pagoda is a tower structure inspired by the stupa.

15. The Great Wall of China was built in stages from about 500 B.C.E. to 1600 C.E. It's the world's largest man-made structure. The wall was designed to discourage Mongol raiders from entering China, Ultimately, the wall failed to prevent Mongol aggression.

16. The Mayan palace and pyramid at Palenque, in the state of Chiapas, Mexico was built about 600 C.E. From the top of the pyramid there is an inside stairway leading down to a chamber built to contain the sarcophagus of a greatly honored king.

17. The Pyramid of the Sun at Teotihuacan, Mexico was built about 100 C.E. It set the pattern for many other religious structures throughout Meso America. Many scholars claim that Teotihuacan was the largest urban center in the pre-Columbian Americas.

18. The Alhambra, Court of Myrtles, was built at Granada, Spain in the 14th century. Its water features must have been a delight for people from arid lands. This fortress was a jewel of Moslem Spain and many of its artistic features influenced generations of Spanish architects.

19. The Dome of the Rock Mosque in Jerusalem was built from 685 to 691 C.E. This mosque rises above the spot where, in Moslem belief, Mohammed ascended to Heaven. This mosque testified to the power of Islam over Jerusalem and the Holy Land.

20. Chartres Cathedral was built about 1194 C.E. It rose 118 feet and had a richly decorated interior. Its spectacular stained glass windows constituted a textbook of glass pages for the religious instruction of illiterate peasants . This method of instruction and indoctrination was used in all the great Gothic cathedrals of Europe.

21. The Piazza del Campo with the Palazzo Pubblico was built in Siena, Italy from 1298 to 1348. The palazzo featured a balcony for speeches undoubtedly meant to transmit persuasive messages to the Sienese citizenry.

22. Angkor Wat is a Hindu complex or religious structures built in Cambodia in the 12th century C.E. It is one of the world's largest ensembles of buildings devoted to religious practices. Today, it is a symbol of Cambodia and is pictured on that nation's national flag.

23. The rock cut Bet Ghiorg (Saint George's) is a church cut out of solid rock in the early 13th century at Lalibela, Ethiopia. St. George is the patron saint of Ethiopia. There are several rock cut churches in Lalibela which are usually subterranean and interconnected.

24. Filippo Bruneleschi designed the dome of Florence Cathedral that when finished became the symbol of the proud city. During the Renaissance many Italian cities competed with each other in the arts and architecture. Construction took place from 1420 to 1436. The cathedral along with its associated structures and art pieces such as Ghiberti's bronze doors , provided instruction in the Catholic faith to the citizens of the city.

25. St. Peter's Basilica in Rome is the largest church in the Christian world. It was built from 1607 to 1612 C.E. Its dome has set the style for many city halls, state capitols and domed churches throughout the world. This church is the symbol of the Vatican and a destination for millions of people from all over the world.

26. The Hall of Prayer for Good Harvests, Temple of Heaven and Earth was built in 1420 C.E. at Beijing. The goal of royal architects was to make humans seem small when gazing up at the structure . The building showed the importance and glory of the Ming (bright) Dynasty.

27. The baroque Church of St. Maria della Salute was built from 1631 to 1687 in Venice. The baroque architectural style was about spectacle, drama, color and bright decorations. The baroque style spread from Italy to the rest of Europe in the 16th , 17th, and 18th centuries. The Roman Catholic Church in sponsoring a Counter-Reformation found that the baroque style could dazzle the masses and help to bring back former Catholics to the Church as well as help in persuading loyal Catholics to stay loyal. This is an outstanding example of the use of architecture as propaganda.

28. St. Peter's Square was built at the Vatican in Rome from 1656 to 1667. The architect Berini wanted to give visitors the impression of being embraced by the arms of the Church. His work created a great public space for thousands of people to hear persuasive messages from the popes.

29. Versailles was the palace of the French kings for many years. It was built over several decades of the 17th and 18th centuries. An estimated

3,000 people , courtiers and others, lived at Versailles. The lords of France and their families were required to live in the palace where they could be spied upon by the king's informers. The guests of the kings were thereby persuaded to avoid angering or plotting against the absolute monarch. Louis XIV has been credited with saying that he was the state. Versailles was just as much an elaborate prison as it was a palatial center of the French government.

30. The Taj Mahal was built at Agra, India from 1630 to 1653. It is a jewel of Islamic architecture and has become a symbol of India.

31. The Eiffel Tower was erected in Paris from 1885 to 1889. This great and innovative iron beam structure persuaded many architects and engineers to explore iron beam construction. The tower reached the height of 1,010 ft. In the beginning of the project the tower was supposed to be a temporary structure but it became a worldwide sensation and subsequently a symbol of both Paris and France.

32. The Pedestal of the Statue of Liberty was built in New York Harbor in 1886. The statue, a gift from France, became a symbol of freedom for millions of immigrants and visitors arriving in America.

33. The Chrysler Building was built from 1928 to 1930 in New York city. The huge skyscraper became a symbol of the growing prestige and power of corporations in American life. Buildings were and still are a major advertising tool.

It was no accident when terrorists on 9/11 successfully destroyed one of America's symbols of its economic power, the World Trade Center. They wanted to destroy the Pentagon, a symbol of America's military power and the Capitol or the White House, both symbols of America's political power. Can anyone deny the propaganda value of many of the world's buildings?

The development of writing vastly increased the progress in about every area of human endeavor. Writing was a major milestone in the human ability to persuade others. No system of writing emerged as a fully organized way of communicating with symbols overnight. Many scholars think that there was a period of proto-writing in which people used symbols and signs and pictures in order to communicate ideas. In the Neolithic (new stone) Age drawings, signs and symbols were carved, picked or otherwise incised on rock surfaces, Such symbols, signs and drawings are called petroglyphs, (rock drawings) .

The first fully developed system of writing appeared somewhere between 5,000 and 6,000 years ago. Mesopotamia and Egypt seem to be places where writing first began. Writing later emerged in the Indus Valley in what is now Pakistan, China and the New World Maya.

In Mesopotamia about the third millennium B.C.E., writing was done by pressing a stylus into the clay in a system called cuneiform. These clay tablets functioned as books. The library of Ashurbanipal at Ninevah, Assyria dated to the 7th century B.C.E. In Egypt , the famous *Book of the Dead* was used by priests in carrying out their funeral duties. There were large libraries of scrolls at Rome and especially at Alexandria, Egypt under the Ptolemaic Dynasty. Hellenistic (Greek-like) Alexandria became the intellectual capital of the Mediterranean world. Large libraries of Buddhist texts were built in China. And the Mayas produced many accordion-like folding books which were, tragically, burned by the Spanish in their conquests of Mexico and Central America. Books in Asia were often made by scribes written on narrow bamboo slats and put together somewhat like a Venetian blind.

The key invention that spread that spread the written word far and wide was printing . Sometime between the 4th and 5th centuries C.E., printing was invented in China. By the 9th century C.E., printed books were appearing in large quantities. There is an existing printed book in China dated at 868 C.E. In the 1040's C.E. the Chinese experimented with moveable type but this was found to be unsuitable given the great number of Chinese characters. In Europe, centuries later, Guttenberg printed a Bible 1453 C.E. European books, at first, were printed on parchment , skin of a sheep or goat, and vellum , a fine parchment of young goat , calf, lamb or kid skin. Parchment and vellum are expensive materials. What the world of printing needed was a cheaper material so that more and more people could purchase and read books. The innovative Chinese came up with the solution – paper. In Europe, paper making became a major industry in Italy in the 13th century C.E. While the Chinese printed newspapers in the 700's C.E., it took the Europeans a much longer time to do so. By the 1700's C.E., newspapers were being published in America. Newspapers in America peaked in 1909 at about 2,000 dailies and about 14,000 weeklies. Newspapers were, for a time, the major source of news and propaganda messages.

Magazines began to enjoy popularity as more and more people learned how to read and at the same time enjoy the increased prosperity produced by a growing industrial economy. The great period of magazine popularity occurred in the late 19th and early 20th centuries. Today, American public opinion is influenced by such magazines as Time, Newsweek and U.S. News and World Report, to name a few.

A dramatic increase in the speed and distance that messages could be delivered was ushered in by the invention of the telegraph. The telegraph foreshadowed telephone communication. The Morse telegraph, which sent messages by wire , was demonstrated in 1837. The Morse Code , a system of dots and dashes, was transmitted throughout the nation and, with the laying of wire cables undersea, throughout the world.

With the coming of television, words and pictures could be transmitted everywhere. Television makes every home a theater. In the late 1800's a German inventor, Paul Gottlieb Nipkow, developed a mechanical scanning device that sent pictures for short distances. In the United States, Philo Farnsworth developed an electronic scanning system in 1922. He first sent pictures electronically in San Francisco, California. In 1923 Vladimir Zworkyn invented his video camera and in 1929 he demonstrated the first practical television system. By 1939 NBC was transmitting the first regular television programs. After the end of World War II, television took off in a big way. Now one can't imagine an American presidential campaign without television. Starting with the Early Bird satellite in 1965, worldwide television became a reality.

A revolution in human affairs occurred with the introduction of the modern computer into our lives. The Z1 was created by the German inventor Konrad Zuse in his parent's living room from 1936 to 1938. His invention is considered to be the first electrical binary programmable computer. The first digital computer was invented by Professor John Vincent and graduate student Cliff Berry at Iowa State University in 1937 and continued to be developed until 1942. In the 1960's and 1970's , the first personal computers entered the marketplace and spread rapidly throughout the world. Written messages raced throughout the planet by e – mail. Every owner of a computer could become a journalist and a persuasive propagandist.

The Internet is a worldwide communication network for the interchange of information. Computer sites all over the earth are joined together. The Defense Department of the United States Government experimented with the connecting of multiple computer sites into a network in 1984. The Internet left the embrace of the Pentagon and rapidly spread throughout the computer world. Computers are the world's greatest propaganda tool in history so far..

CHAPTER 7

WHAT ARE SOME OFTEN OVERLOOKED FORMS OF PROPAGANDA?

There are so many tools that can be used for propaganda that it's hard to know where to begin. The following forms, the tip of the ice berg , are just a few that I have come upon in my studies. In previous writings in this book I have discussed the importance of human speech, writing, art, architecture, inventions and persuasive personalities. I hope that the reader will expand the list to include his or her own observations.

- Music has been used since the stone age to prepare warriors for combat. Napoleon led his troops into battle accompanied by a military band. In hospitals music is played to try to calm patients. When I sailed to Europe on the Flandre, a French liner, the band played the Battle Hymn of the Republic and northerners stood up to sing the lyrics. This was followed by the song Dixie and southerners rose to the call with much emotion.
- Insignias are used for propaganda purposes throughout the world. The Jewish Star of David, the Christian cross, the Islamic crescent, the Hindu wheel of life, the yin – yang of Taoism and the Nazi swastika which was seen in much of Europe for a thankfully brief period, are all examples of powerful insignias. Medals can be mentioned here, Napoleon reportedly said that if you give a man a medal he'll die for it.

- Mascots are usually seen as representative of schools, colleges and universities . They are especially noticeable at sports events. The Russian bear, the American eagle, the British lion and the Chinese dragon are just a few examples of national mascots.
- Banners in the form of flags are patriotic symbols that can be used to arouse nationalistic feelings as well as to stife opposition to a government's policies, especially in its foreign affairs.
- Coins, stamps and bumper stickers are often used for propaganda purposes. The currency of the United States has the phrase IN GOD WE TRUST inscribed on it. This was most likely done in response to the horrendous loss of life during the catastrophic Civil War. American presidents are conspicuous role models and appear on both coins, stamps and currency.. Pledges and oaths have great power to shape thoughts and behavior. The American pledge of allegiance has the phrase under God in it as a result of the Cold War competition between the godless Soviet Union and the God respecting United States. Oaths were so important in the German army that many officers who opposed Hitler refused to enter into any plots for his downfall because they took an oath of loyalty to him. During the McCarthy era in in the postwar United States a loyalty oath became a way to silence any voices that could be linked to supposedly communist ideas.
- Rituals, rites and spectacles are seen in all cultures. Egyptian funeral processions , Chinese imperial spectacles, Roman triumphal celebrations and Nazi Nuremberg rallies and British royal coronations are examples of a great propaganda tool.
- Plays, skits and satirical presentations of humorous commentators bring drama into the world of propaganda. The play *Uncle Tom's Cabin* helped to turn many Americans against the institution of slavery.
- Clothing has been used since the cave days and is a major tool of propaganda in most societies. The crowns of the Egyptian pharaohs, Rome's imperial purple togas, the Chinese imperial silk robes, English judges big wigs, military uniforms, top hats and tails and Ku Klux Klan robes and head masks are just a few examples of how humans try to influence others with clothing. We humans often wear propaganda.

- Gestures have propaganda value. The V sign for victory made by spreading apart two fingers of the hand was a popular American morale builder during World War II. Military salutes, politicians happy waves accompanied by a big smile, taking off hats as a sign of respect and, in the United States, holding the hand over the heart in the pledge of allegiance are all examples.

- Behavior that sets an example has a long history. Confucius put great store in setting an example to show others how to behave. In the Roman Catholic tradition, saints certainly are thought to set an example for the faithful. In the Pacific theater at the last days of World War II , Japan was clearly losing the conflict. A Japanese naval officer who thought that suicide bombing could turn things around, disobeyed orders and crashed his plane into an American ship. The example he set helped to create a Kamikaze Corps of suicide pilots that caused many American casualties.

- Displays are an ancient form of propaganda. Even our cousins, the chimpanzees, stage displays of strength to win the respect of others. In 1854, Commodore Perry displayed the power of the American navy and showed off what were the technological wonders of his day to the Japanese. These displays are credited with opening up Japan to international trade and formal relations between America and Japan. Later in American history President Theodore Roosevelt sent the Great White Fleet on a world tour to show off the strength of his nation's fleet. The U.S. Air Force uses the Blue Angels to display the talents of their pilots and win over some future recruits.

- Gift giving often has propaganda strings attached to it. Some churches who provide free meals to needy people include sermons in the menu. The strings attached to a gift are revealed when the recipients of a gift feel obliged to carry out the wishes of the gift giver. The potlatch ceremonies of some Pacific Northwest Native Americans involved gift giving to enhance the prestige of the gift giver. Big donors to the electoral campaigns of politicians often have strings attached to their gifts. They usually want to influence legislation to favor their goals.

- College degrees and professional credentials and licenses are often persuasive propaganda tools. I'm fairly sure that most people feel more secure when the college degrees on the office wall of their doctor have been granted from prestigious institutions.

- The human body has been used as a propaganda tool for ages. The fine bodies of athletes of the Nordic variety were glorified in the German film *Olympia* produced at the time of the 1936 Olympic games in Nazi Berlin. The splendid performance of the African – American athlete, Jessie Owens damaged the master race idea so dear to Adolf Hitler. When I was studying the California missions I noticed a skull embedded in a wall, I was told that this was to show that death is near for all of us and that we should work to deserve our entrance into Heaven. The female body has been used in advertising because sex sells.

- Telemarketing is a method of direct marketing in which a salesperson solicits to prospective customers to buy products or services , either over the phone or through a subsequent face to face or Web conferencing appointment scheduled during the call. Some people date the beginnings of telemarketing back to the 1950's.

- Chambers of commerce are found in almost every sizeable community. Their major goal is to stimulate business activity in their community and to serve as centers for tourist information. Chambers of commerce could easily be called chambers of persuasion.

- We are a mobile society so it's no surprise that ads are painted on automobiles, busses and street cars. In political campaigns people with bull horns drive around neighborhoods delivering propaganda supporting the candidates who generally pay for their services.

- Mathematics is a field that can be used as a propaganda tool. Graphs in particular can be designed to support the goals and wishes of the government or corporation sponsoring the creation of the graph. Numbers can be made to lie so watch out.

- Dance has been an important tool of propaganda in several nations. In the Soviet Union, dance troops would attract onlookers and then would come the propaganda messages. In China, especially during the time of Chairman Mao, music and dance performances were featured in plays written to support the policies of the ruling party.

- Humor is a great propaganda tool. Humor comes in many forms: bathos, pathos, burlesque, caricature, hyperbole, irony, mimicry, oxymoron, parody, personification, ridicule, sarcasm, satire etc. Satire, making fun of what you want to attack, is a common feature in political propaganda.
- Sports are a persuader's dream. Sporting events are perhaps the most popular pastime for people all over the world. We tend to make heroes out of successful athletes in our major spectator sports such as football and baseball. Corporations pay large sums of money to sports figures who endorse their products.

Chapter 8

WHO USES PROPAGANDA?

There is an easy answer to the question of who uses propaganda – everybody uses propaganda at one time or another. We are all faced with making choices in life: Will I seek a divorce or try to work things out?, Should I buy a new car or have another child?, Should I give my money to charity or keep it for myself?, or as a first time politician, Should I admit that I'm an atheist or should I go to church , with a Bible in my hand and look for a photo opportunity? In all these cases the individual would wind up using propaganda on his or her self. It's the old story of a bad angel whispering into one ear while a good angel whispers into the other ear.

The family is a powerful propaganda agency. As a teacher for fifty years, I've observed that my observant Jewish students had one or both observant Jewish parents. Also, my Christian church going students had parents who also were church going folks. The same could be said of Buddhist, Hindu ot Islamic students. It's like an old saying, "the apple doesn't fall far from the tree". What's going on here is that many parents are trying to persuade their children to follow parental values, attitudes and behaviors.. It seems that some parents would like to have their children be intellectual clones of themselves.

Many religious organizations use a variety of persuasive techniques to indoctrinate their members, especially their young ones. Religious holidays, rites of passage (birth, wedding and death), routine prayers, etc. Most religious leaders know that constant reinforcement of a person's faith is necessary in order to maintain it. They also know that young children are most receptive to propaganda messages. The Nazis knew this too and they organized the Hitler Youth group. Many young Germans felt that it was an honor to die for the Fuhrer.

We learn the most important information in our adapting to our culture into which we were born, as children. We don't choose our culture but we have to try to live successfully in it. In a way we are all trapped within a cultural blueprint that we had no part in designing.

If we look at social organizations, we see that special interest groups have proliferated in the modern world. Donation requests fill most people's mail boxes as all special interest groups appear to need money to thrive or simply survive. It would be interesting to see a list of all special interest groups but few have the time for such a lengthy investigation. I have selected a few groups to mention:

- The American Medical Association works to benefit its members in the medical professions. The AMA is a strong lobbying force in both state and national legislatures.
- The Knights of Columbus is a fraternal organization of Roman Catholic men who work to support the values of their faith. They donate funds to support or oppose proposed laws.
- The American Association of Retired People AARP, works to further the interests of retirees and senior citizens as well.

The economic sphere is a huge arena for propagandists. In a capitalist society large corporations have major interests in one thing – profits. Profits are mainly tied to an ever growing economy. To promote growth it is necessary to spend billions of dollars on advertising. People need to be made to feel that they need goods and services that they may not really need. Happiness, contentment and lack of greed and envy are toxic elements in a consumer based economic system. Advertisers know this and they spend considerable efforts to stimulate feelings of greed and envy in their advertisements. In today's world you can seldom ever be out of reach of advertising. Newspapers, magazines, radio and television stations, sign boards and computers are always full of commercials aimed at reducing the money supply of the consumer. To be fair, some advertising provides good information and gives consumers some facts and figures that may help in choosing goods and services. It is also true that when consumption declines unemployment usually follows which can result in recessions and depressions. The number of persuaders employed in the advertising industry is impressive, but we need this army of propagandists to keep a capitalist society in good economic health.

In our society's political sphere propaganda is a dominant element in the attainment and transfer of power. Lobbyists, often paid persuaders, try to influence legislators and administrators at the local, state and national levels. Politicians listen to people who can make financial contributions to their campaigns for reelection. Political campaigns are horrendously expensive. Also, sometimes if a politician dismisses an important lobbyist that person may choose to support the politician's opponent in the next election.

Political parties spend billions of dollars to try to win the votes of the electorate to assure the victory of their candidates running for office. Rallies, fund raising banquets, badges, signs, banners, bumper stickers, huge party convention ending with a show of balloons , mailings and television and radio ads are just some of the money gobbling tools used by political parties to persuade voters. Elected officials, once in office, usually begin to use propaganda to plan for the next election.

The departments and agencies of local, state and national governments are also big users of propaganda in their attempts to influence the citizenry. To offer one example, the national Defense Department strongly supports the policies and actions of the administration of which it is a part. It uses persuasion, both at home and abroad, to advance the goals of the president. Army recruiting advertisements have recently announced, "Join the Army and be all you can be." Two things you can be are wounded and killed but this isn't mentioned of course.

To sum things up, propaganda and persuasion are ubiquitous in all aspects of life.

Chapter 9

WHAT MIGHT BE THE FUTURE OF PROPAGANDA?

This brief chapter is an exercise in pure speculation but here goes:

1. Subliminal suggestion may become a sneaky way to influence minds. Working on the subconscious will be of great concern.

2. Computer chips implanted in people's brains may be able to control thoughts.

3. Computer virtual reality may become a major propaganda tool.

4. Brain imaging technology may be used to discover your true thoughts. Lie detecting may be vastly improved,

5. Digital photography may give birth to a new saying based on an old one – "a picture is worth a thousand lies.

6. *1984*, Orwell's dystopian novel, may come to pass and we'll see history rewritten.

7. Propaganda messages will be increasingly tailored to many specific audiences.

8. Digital television might lend itself to the manipulation and distortion of images to achieve the goals of propagandists.

9. Blogging, which is basically writing a journal on the Internet, will increase greatly. Anyone with a computer and access to the Internet, will be able to be an editorial writer with a worldwide audience.

10. Some "think tanks" might morph into "propaganda tanks"

11. Lobbying might continue at an even greater scale than ever.

12. Primate studies might aid in determining human behavior patterns which would be welcomed by persuaders of all stripes.

13. The greatest persuasion industry, advertising, might continue to grow for it is the engine that drives a consumer society. An estimated 70% of the American economy is fueled by consumer spending.

14. Propaganda may increasingly be masqueraded as news, especially from governmental sources.

CHAPTER 10

WHAT ARE SOME PROPAGANDA TECHNIQUES?

Propaganda techniques are the tools of all persuaders. The number of such techniques is staggering. The hundred techniques that are presented in this chapter are just a few that I have selected. New techniques appear every year. Writers of persuasive messages should find these techniques to be useful but my big hope is that people who are interested in developing their critical thinking skills will be forewarned and therefore forearmed against bad propaganda messages.

I have placed the propaganda into 7 sections as Follows:

1. Techniques of Faulty Logic

2. Techniques of Diversion or Evasion

3. Techniques That Appeal to the Emotions

4. Techniques that involve Fallacies or Trickery

5. Techniques That Play on Human Behavioral Tendencies

6. Techniques of Style

7. Techniques of Reason and Common Sense

The exercises included in this chapter are designed to be used in classes on critical thinking.p

SECTION 1 – TECHNIQUES OF FAULTY LOGIC

SIMPLIFICATION

It's faulty reasoning to imagine that the simplification of a complex idea, issue or problem can be done without sacrificing some content and understanding of the message. This being said, it is often necessary for a propagandist to simplify complexities in order to have even the skeleton of his or her ideas understood and accepted.

Simplification can reach a broad audience for several reasons. Complex messages take time to fully comprehend and when people are rushed, they tend to ignore what is being said. Another reason for a propagandist to simplify some idea or issue is to reach an audience with poor language skills.

When a bank sponsors a commercial that states, "...all your troubles will be over when you take out a loan with us", simplification is at work.

A propagandist must be careful in using the simplification technique with a sophisticated audience that might fell that he or she was being condescending.

One way to easily simplify a message is to check the vocabulary being used. Foreign words or phrases, which might not be widely known, will be omitted and complex words will be replaced with simpler words more easily understood.

CONCURRENCY

This is one of a group of illogical propaganda techniques still being widely used. Its form is usually stated in this way: A with B, therefore A cause of B. When a propagandist has a clearly defined goal he or she can often use concurrency to either support something wanted or attack something unwanted.

Let's say there is a builder of tract houses. The propagandist wants to present reasons to a town council in support of a proposed project. Using concurrency an attempt is made to make as many associations as possible between the proposed project and various positive factors or trends in the target community. If economic conditions are good in the area, the builder attempts to show a causal relationship between home construction and a booming economy. The builder will say that home construction and general prosperity walk hand in hand.

In another example of concurrency, let's say a propagandist is opposed to motion pictures with explicit sexual themes being shown where he or she lives. The propagandist begins to research what's going on in the community looking for negative data to support the position being advocated. Statistics on unwed mothers, abandoned newborn babies, sexual crimes such as rape or pederasty will be gathered. In trying to make causal connections between motion picture content and the negative data the propagandist has gathered, he or she will try to persuade others that censorship of such films is necessary.

POST HOC

This technique follows the pattern that A precedes B, therefore A is the cause of B.

As an example let's imagine a hypothetical nation somewhere in the mid-Pacific Ocean. We can picture a place which is run by two political parties; party one and party two. An advocate of the party might claim that a great war occurred when party two was at the helm and would try to link that war with the foreign policy of party two. In fact, there might not be any provable relationship.

On the other hand, an advocate of party two might say that a great economic depression occurred while party one ran the nation and would try to link the economic depression with the economic policies of party one. Here also there might not be any provable relationship.

Any time a driven propagandist can associate something negative with someone or something he or she doesn't like, the temptation to use a post hoc argument is difficult to resist.

GENERALIZATION

A generalization can be identified as having the following form: A1 is B, A2 is B, A3 is B, therefore all As are B. An example would be that if you know an Italian professor who is intelligent, an Italian judge who is intelligent and an Italian doctor who is intelligent you might conclude that all Italians are intelligent. It may be said that this line of reasoning is ridiculous but generalizations such as the example given pass for reasoning every day in some circles.

Any time a propagandist says the words all, none or never, a listener or reader can suspect that an error is being made. It only takes one exception to disprove a generalization. If *most* is substituted for *all* there will still be the burden of proving that 50% + 1 of all Italians are intelligent. A safer way out of these burdens is to say that *some* Italians are intelligent. Statements with the word some are usually weak.

Like it or not, we all tend to generalize at times because we haven't got the time to explore things thoroughly. If you purchase three apples from a store barrel and they're all rotten you tend to feel that the whole barrel is full of rotten apples. You may be right or you may be wrong but why take a chance? This is how generalizations get their power to convince.

FAULTY ANALOGY

An analogy is a correspondence in some respects between things otherwise dissimilar, such as "a ninety year old and a twelve year old both like to swim?. They have love of a sport in common, but not physical capabilities.

The more dissimilar things being compared are the more faulty the analogy. If a Navy poster claimed that it as safer to be in the Navy than to be a resident of New York City, the analogy would be quite faulty. The Navy would be comparing death rates that are not comparable. Only generally young and healthy men and women are admitted into the Navy while New York City has the complete range humans from babies to senior citizens. When a Navy person gets old or severely ill he or she is discharged and returns to the general population. Of course the death rate is greater in New York City than in the Navy, but such an argument, while rather silly, might be persuasive to many young people.

CONDEMNING THE ORIGIN

This technique attempts to discredit an idea by showing that it has an unappealing source.

One example of this technique would be a claim made by an advocate for the abolition of the death penalty. Such a claim might sound like this; 'The prison system and capital punishment are children of the Dark Ages and should be abolished'.

Another example comes from the history of Nazi Germany. Adolf Hitler was not receptive to any proposals from his scientists for embarking on a nuclear bomb project. He considered nuclear physics to bed a "Jewish" science. Any German scientist who showed respect for people like Albert Einstein, a Jew, would be labeled as a "white Jew". In Hitler's condemnation of the source of scientific ideas about nuclear weapons, he ignored what would be the greatest secret weapon of World War II.

I can remember hearing people condemn our use of Dr. Werner von Braun for his ideas and organizing ability in America's guided missile development program on the grounds that the good doctor was Adolf Hitler's rocket scientist.

FALSE CONVERSION OF PROPOSITIONS

A propagandist will start with a true proposition and end up with one that does not follow. A person who states that all communists are atheists and goes on to say that therefore all atheists are communists is demonstrating the use of this technique.

The statement, "All Roman Catholics believe in God", followed by "All those people who believe in God are Roman Catholics." would probably not be as easily accepted as the first example might be.

WHAT IS TRUE OF THE PARTS IS TRUE OF THE WHOLE

This is an old logical fallacy that continues to be used today. Let's say that a hater of a governor of one of America's states wants to get him out of office. The hater could search out a few negative features of the governor's administration and go on to draw the conclusion that the governor deserved to be recalled from office.

An automobile salesperson might put down a competitor's car by selecting a few weaknesses in the car and drawing the conclusion that it's a lemon.

Taking a different slant on things a Neo-Nazi could argue that Adolf Hitler loved animals, especially his dog, was loyal to his friends such as Benito Mussolini and won a medal for bravery in World War I (a German Jewish officer recommended Adolf for an iron cross). When the Neo-Nazi claims that these facts show how good and great the Fuhrer was you would most likely hold your nose. The fact is that this is an extreme example of the fallacy. This technique might get a better reception if it were used against or for someone less well known.

THE BLACK AND WHITE FALLACY

A statement that doesn't allow for intermediate states between two extremes is often a black and white fallacy.

For instance, if people are being described as being good or bad, patriotic or unpatriotic, skinny or fat, tall or short, having thick hair or being bald, a believer or infidel, for or against, just or unjust or happy or sad, the propagandist is using this black and white fallacy.

Of course there are some polarized terms that are valid. For instance a woman is either pregnant or not pregnant. A man or woman is either dead or alive.

USING AN ILLICIT DEFINITION

This technique involves using a word that has an old and accepted definition and giving the word a new and often unrecognized definition.

Examples:

> "If you have an abortion and terminate the life of a potential human being, you are guilty of murder." This use of the word "murder" is flaunting the accepted legal definition.

> Alcohol is a drug and anyone selling it is a drug dealer. Liquor store owners should be imprisoned." Here the propagandist is trying to confuse the issue. Alcohol is not an illegal drug in the United States, whereas some other drugs are.

FALLACY OF BIASED SAMPLING

A propagandist may issue millions of questioners but if his or her sampling is biased, there'll be misleading results. This may lead to false conclusions.

In 1936, before the presidential election, the Reader's Digest magazine distributed millions of questioners in order to attempt to forecast whether Landon or Roosevelt would win the upcoming contest. Peoples' names and addresses were randomly chosen from telephone directories and club membership lists.

In the Great Depression period, many people didn't have telephones and weren't listed in the telephone directories, weren't members of clubs and therefore weren't contacted. This group of urban and rural poor overwhelmingly supported Roosevelt.

Some 2 ½ million responses to the Reader's Digest questioners were received by the magazine, all indicating a Landon victory. he magazine predicted a win by Landon over Roosevelt. It didn't happen – Roosevelt won. The biased sampling was flawed making the results invalid. The Reader's Digest lost a great degree of its former credibility due to careless sampling.

A propagandist might still go ahead and conduct a biased poll in which the responses would have been designed to support the propagandist's position. The attempt to influence others in this way would be just one of many examples of the principle of using any means to achieve the desired end.

THE GAMBLER'S FALLACY

People often reason that if they've had a spell of bad luck, they should increase their bets. They feel this way because they assume that they are due for a spell of good luck to balance things out.

A propagandist can make use of the Gambler's Fallacy. If you are running for high office against an opponent who has experienced a run of bad luck, or has made unfortunate mistakes you have an opportunity. You can shout to your audience that you'll change things and bring back happy days. You might say that it's about time that the people's fortunes were changed. You could add to this by saying that we all certainly deserve a win after a series of losses. You will hope that the people will go for this message just like some gamblers do.

THE FALLACY OF INCONSISTENCY

This fallacy of inconsistency occurs when we reason from inconsistent premises.

Example:

> When a propagandist claims that a fetus is a person with an absolute right to life and goes on to say that an abortion is morally wrong except in cases of rape and incest, he or she is reasoning from inconsistent premises.

APPEAL TO INAPPROPRIATE AUTHORITY

When alleged experts are not in a position to know or are otherwise unreliable, the propagandist is appealing to inappropriate authority.

In the mass media this technique is being used quite often. In a commercial designed to encourage people to drink beer, a movie star or athlete will beat out a brew master every time in touting the greatness of the beverage.

CLAIM GAIN WITH NO PAIN

This is the standard argument of many advertisers. The prospective buyer is told that he or she can have a luxury automobile for pennies a day or buy a new home with a very low down payment. Buyers beware! Politicians often promise new services with no new taxes. The voters should know better.

SECTION 2 – TECHNIQUES OF DIVERSION OR EVASION

USE OF AMBIGUOUS WORDS

An ambiguous word is one that is susceptible of multiple interpretations. Words such as God, good, freedom, democracy and truth can have many different meanings. By failing to properly define terms, a propagandist can appear to be saying something very concrete when in fact he or she may be saying little of substance. People tend to supply their own definitions of terms and can readily be taken in by a manipulating speaker or writer.

In the statement, "John Smith is a very good candidate," critical thinkers should want some serious discussion of exactly what is meant by the word good.

I once went to a meeting in a church held by a prominent anticommunist organization. The speaker featured at this evening event, open to the public, was an enthusiastic opponent of communism. When question time came around, I asked the speaker if he would kindly define the word communist. He didn't answer that question. I had the feeling that he wanted to be able to label anyone or anything he didn't like as communist.

Quite often a propagandist can get away with using ambiguous words and their use is alive and well to judge from observing the mass media.

AD HOMINEM

In Latin ad hominem means "to the man". In today's world it means "to attack a person with words". This technique calls for the abandonment of reason in argument and instead attacking the character of a person. If carried to an extreme, it often results in a poor outcome for the user. Engaging in ad hominem attacks is often referred to as mud slinging.

BEGGING THE QUESTION

Begging the question assumes that something not yet proven is true. If the audience lets the propagandist get away with it, begging the question can be an effective technique.

Some Examples:

> "Our founding fathers would have never supported the regulation of firearms." (How do we know what the founding fathers would or would not have supported?)

> "The future course America must follow is technology, technology, and ever more technology" (The speaker must be pressed to offer some evidence in support of his or her claim.)

"God is on our side." (Prove this and you've done the impossible!)

> "History has shown that we must make preemptive strikes against our enemies." (History shows us very little.)

In all of these statements the conclusions are subject to the rigors of proof. Of course the propagandist will conveniently pay no mind to this requirement of critical thinking.

THE WICKED ALTERNATIVE

Using this technique the propagandist tries to defend someone or something by attacking its opposite.

A propagandist who proclaimed that "We must immediately undertake a massive program of building both a light and a heavy railway system as well as subway systems in all the large cities" will support his position by attacking private transportation. He or she might claim that our present "car culture", with its millions of automobiles, has given us great numbers of deaths and horrible injuries. Continuing the attack, the propagandist might claim that the medical system has been severely stressed. The pollution problem and the waste of much good land for ever growing highway systems might also be advanced.

Sometimes propagandists will set up a decoy, either a person or a thing, that is made to seem so bad and unacceptable that the alternative, backed by the propagandist, looks good. If a real estate salesperson shows you a terrible high priced house that is being used as a decoy, that next house you see may look so much better than the first that you unthinkingly reach for your checkbook.

NON-SEQUITUR

Non-sequitur is a diversionary technique in which a person seems to e answering a question but, in fact, isn't. Imagine a mother wanting to know what went on during her daughter's first date:

> Mother: "How was your date with Harry?"
>
> Daughter: "Mom, you should have seen Harry's car! Dad would have loved it. It had a television in the back and four loudspeakers for the stereo. To ride in that car was like riding on a cloud."

In this exchange it's doubtful that the mother was concerned about Harry's car. She was trying to find out about other matters and her daughter knew it.

ACCUSING THE ACCUSER

This is a way to attempt to fend off an attack by making a diversion. The minute the propagandist is accused of something, he or she fires off a counter accusation.

Example:

> Senator A: "You spend too much of the taxpayers' money"!

> Senator B: "What about that fact finding trip you and your wife took to Europe?"

NAME CALLING

This is an unsophisticated and demeaning technique to use. It is used by propagandists who feel that their audience is made up of simple minded, rather unthinking people. I recommend not using this technique but in its stead offer reasons and evidence that support your views.

Dr. Josef Goebbels the Nazi propaganda chief used name-calling against Jews in Germany and throughout the world. He labeled Jews as "untermenschen" or sub-humans. The Nazis didn't have an exclusive ownership of this technique. Winston Churchill, the Prime Minister of Great Britain during World War II, called Hitler a "bloodthirsty gutter snipe."

People, places and things have been the recipients of this primitive name-calling technique. (By the way, my use of the word primitive to describe this technique could be labeled as name-calling.)

Some Examples of Name-Calling:

For People:	dirty rat, black dog, vermin, vipers, gutter snipes, uncouth, vulgar, crude, Neanderthal, scum, slime ball, jerk, idiot, imbecile, bitch, witch, fool
For Places:	Hell hole, the pits, a dump, the boondocks, a jungle, a snake pit, a shark tank, the sticks, a mud hole, a slum, no place, a zoo. an insane asylum
For Things:	Outrageous, primitive, crude, ugly, useless, horrible, nasty, inferior, stupid, bizarre, ridiculous, a "rube goldberg"

THE USE OF SATIRE

Satire is attacking human vices and follies through wit. Satire is used to attack those conventional ideas and practices that are thought to be absurdities in the opinion of the satirist. The vices usually chosen as targets by satirists are those considered to be blindly accepted by people through thoughtlessness, habit or social custom. The distance between how things are and how they should be is revealed by the satirist.

A few subjects for satire are prejudice, lack of foresight, quest for total security, war, crime, cruelty, impatience, disloyalty, pride, sloth, lust, envy, greed, anger, gluttony and the list goes on.

An example of satirical writing which attacks the folly of an individual's search for extreme personal security is shown in the following essay.

SECURITY FOREVER

Justin Smythe lived in a very large American city and he was scared out of his wits. The crime rate in his town was high and steadily increasing. He saw himself and his family in extreme danger.

Justin went on to make a decision to do something to protect himself and his family from evil doers. He installed a television camera to constantly sweep the area in front of his house. He was especially proud of the expert way he placed two automatic 50 caliber machine guns to cover his front door. Land mines were cleverly placed under the front lawn. "Flame throwers" would get anyone foolishly attempting to climb an exterior wall. The backyard was the perfect place for his six pit traps with sharp spears embedded in their bases – a little something along with jungle fever that he picked on his stint in Vietnam. Barbed wire supplemented the electrified fence that was protecting the rear of the property. Bulletproof glass as used to replace the ordinary windowpanes.

All of these security systems weren't cheap. There as no more going out to restaurants, movies, concerts or taking vacations. Even ordering a pizza was out of the question, but for a different reason!

There were some savings at first. The family dog Bonzo fell into one of the backyard pits while he was chasing a cat. That ended the purchasing of pet food and paying for a yearly license. Things got a little rough when Justin's mother-in-law made an unannounced visit and was cut down by the two machine guns at the front door. When the mailperson stepped on a front lawn land mine, Justin was arrested, tried and thrown into prison for a long stretch.

The lawsuits that followed le to some more unfortunate incidents in Justin's life. He was forced sell his house and surrender his life savings. His wife divorced him and the kids don't come to visit daddy. However, there's one bright spot in all of these happenings. He doesn't worry too much about intruders where he lives now.

REPARTEE

Repartee is an exchange of quick witty replies to sharp or bitter remarks. Only outstandingly clever propagandists should try this technique.

Examples:

Gladstone vs. Disraeli (members of the British government)

Gladstone: "You'll either die from a hangman's noose or from a social disease."

Disraeli: "That depends on whether I embrace your principles or your mistress."

Lady Nancy Astor, who entered the House of Commons in 1919 as its first woman member, had few betters in the art of vicious repartee. But she did have some and Winston Churchill was one of them. After one conflict over ideas, Lady Astor is reported to have said to Churchill, "Winston, if you were my husband, I would poison your coffee." Churchill replied, "If you were my wife, Nancy, I would drink it."

Reportedly, Isadora Duncan approached George Bernard Shaw with the proposal that they should have a child. She thought that the combination of her looks and his brains would be impressive. Shaw supposedly countered by saying that it might go the other way – her brains and his looks.

CHOOSE A SCAPEGOAT

Scapegoat is a term used to focus the blame, correctly or incorrectly, on one group. History is strewn with groups used as scapegoats, especially ethnic, religious, racial or social class. These groups were blamed for all or most of the ills of a particular society.

In Nazi Germany, Jews became the scapegoats for that nation's numerous problems. In Turkey during the period of World War I, Armenian Christians were blamed for that nation's troubles. In Indonesia, especially after World War II, Chinese were blamed for troubles. Many African tribal groups in South Africa blamed Hindus for economic problems. In the United States the Ku Klux Klan blamed Jews, Catholics and others for all of Americas problems. The list of scapegoats seems endless.

A propagandist can set up a scapegoat to take the blame for almost any problem. Here is a list of some common problems accompanied by their related scapegoats:

High prices: corporate greed, labor unions demand for higher wages

Poor medical care: drug companies, greedy doctors

Suburban sprawl: white flight, land developers, highway interests

Environmental problems: overpopulation, the automobile, big business

Almost any problem you can think of has more than one cause. Blaming one thing for a problem is a way of diverting attention from what may be the actual cause or causes of the problem

SECTION 3 – TECHNIQUES THAT APPEAL TO THE EMOTION

APPEAL TO TRADITION

This technique appeals to people who use historical precedent to judge ideas. All of us , at some point, have heard people say, "But we've always done it that way." This attitude works against innovation and change.

Here are two examples of the use of this technique:

Those who are against gun control could argue that our founding fathers would have fought any attempts to restrict the use of firearms.

Military historians often remark that nations are usually prepared for the next war based on what went on in the last war. Many times these nations are caught off guard by innovations. Adolf Hitler felt that the air force should be built around fighter planes as in World War I. He felt that jet planes were a waste of time. The world might have been in for sad times if the Fuhrer hadn't been so tradition bound.

Have we outgrown appeals to tradition? Certainly not and a propagandist can often get loud applause by appealing to the values that sustained our nation through good and bad times in the past.

DEMAND FOR SPECIAL CONSIDERATION

This technique is usually based on a hardship story. Politicians and lawyers are well known for making pleas for special circumstances to get someone or something off the hook.

The following is a list of selected areas from which hardship stories may emerge:

Gender, race, political groups, religion, mental or physical disabilities, height, weight, social class, regional background, sexual orientation, occupation, past record or behavior, temporary mental state, membership in an organization etc.

A politician might argue that strong gun controls would constitute a hardship on farmers and ranchers who cannot protect their crops and herds from predators without the unrestricted purchase and use of firearms.

You can imagine a lawyer arguing for a lighter sentence for his client based on that client's past good behavior. The lawyer might claim that a severe sentence would be truly hard on a person who has only slipped once from the straight and narrow path.

APPEAL TO THE EMOTIONS

Human emotions constitute a very complex set of feelings. The range of emotions is extensive and each emotion can be subdivided into seemingly endless variations.

Emotions can be compared to colors. A person can choose one color and by adding increasing amounts of white he or she can create endless tints of color. If a person adds increasing amounts of black to the chosen color he or she can create endless shades of the color.

Love can be subdivided into compassion, fondness, obsessive attachment, adoration and so forth. Fear can be subdivided into terror, apprehension, uneasiness and countless phobias attached to an infinite list of objects and situations.

One way of thinking about emotions is to list some of them under two headings: Positive Emotions and Negative Emotions.

Positive Emotions: love, hope, faith, enthusiasm, loyalty, pity, remorse, etc.

Negative Emotions: unreasonable fear, jealousy, anger, revenge, greed, envy, arrogance, etc.

Let's look at four examples that involve an appeal to the emotions.

An Appeal for Pity

Humans are capable of feeling pity or sympathy for the misfortunes of others. A lawyer can tap into this feeling and often get a jury to either reduce his or her client's sentence or possibly acquit him or her.

Demonstrating that a murderer had an abusive childhood is not an unusual ploy used by lawyers in the nation's courtrooms. This appeal will seldom work if the plea for mercy doesn't have some basis in fact that makes the appeal seem reasonable. An accused murderer of his parents might make a plea for mercy on the grounds that he or she is now orphaned but it would most likely meet with rejection by the average jury.

There are two famous appeals for pity made by American political leaders.

In 1944, some republicans accused President Roosevelt of sending a heavy destroyer to the Aleutian Islands to pick up his pet dog Fala, a Scottish terrier. The president was outraged and made a speech in which he said something to the effect that he and his family didn't resent attacks but his little dog Fala did. Republican critics were silenced by the sympathetic response of the American people.

In 1952, Richard Nixon was accused by Democrats of dipping into a party "slush fund" for personal expenses. Some of his fellow Republicans thought a scandal was in the making. To save his vice-presidential candidacy, Nixon made a speech on September 23, 1952 defending himself by saying he hadn't been feathering his own nest. He acknowledged receiving several gifts which could be returned, but he vowed to keep Checkers, a cocker spaniel that was a gift to his daughters. The American public felt sympathetic to him and he went on to become the vice-president. This became known as the "Checkers Speech".

An Appeal Based on remorse:

A lawyer can try to show his or her client has remorse for the crime he or she has committed. Sometimes this will sway the jury resulting in a lighter sentence for the accused. You'll see this technique in any visit to a criminal court.

An Appeal to Greed:

Greed seems to be a universal characteristic of people everywhere. A mayor of a small town with economic problems might request the community's support for constructing a prison. The mayor might claim that new jobs would be created, taxes would be lowered and town businesses would profit by the expected increase in economic activity brought about by the new prison. The opposition to the project would have a hard time fighting the mayor, I suspect.

An Appeal to Fear:

Fear is one of the most basic emotional states. It is an excellent choice for any propagandist's appeal to emotions. A Xenophobic politician might argue that we should seal off our borders to immigrants before Americans become overrun by foreigners who don't share our values, don't act within the law and take jobs from our children.

To witness a play on several emotions simultaneously, one only has to observe the behavior of apocalyptic cults. These "end of the world" groups are usually always after recruits and their group leaders generally play on fear but at the same time offer hope, meaning and purpose.

Vulnerable people seeking a firm foundation of belief in something greater than themselves are often taken in by these cults.

Once recruited the cult leaders often work on feelings of shame and/or guilt in order to manipulate (brainwash) members. This approach can work with all groups, not just apocalyptic cults. A salesperson offering a set of encyclopedias, or encyclopedia software, can use shame/guilt to encourage parents to buy things for the benefit of their children. Adolf Hitler used the shame of German's defeat in World War I to move his audiences. The American president, J. F. Kennedy, said in his inaugural address of January 20, 1961, "...ask not what your country can do for you – ask what you can do for your country." He was using shame/guilt to try to motivate his fellow Americans.

An effective propagandist, appealing to the emotions, deliberately shows his or her emotional feelings to an audience. If the propagandist is delivering an uplifting speech, a show of joy and enthusiasm is in order. If a somber message filled with warnings and dire predictions of a hazardous future is being given, then the emotions of the propagandist must credibly support the necessary mood of sadness, doom and gloom.

People generally like to see a speaker who displays an emotional commitment to the ideas, issues and principles being transmitted to listeners and/or readers.

PERSONIFICATION

Personification is giving human characteristics to something that is non-human.

In World War II, American propaganda posters portrayed Japanese soldiers as large rats eagerly feeding on the victims of their conquests. They were giving the rats the characteristics of an enemy.

In advertising there are numerous animals given the power of speech. When some young children see a pet Chihuahua they expect it to speak. Dogs speak in the television commercials don't they?

> A n environmentalist might say that acid rain is whispering in our ears, "Take care of the environment or the environment will take care of you."

THE USE OF HOT AND COLD WORDS

Emotion packed words or, as I call them, hot words, carry great power to arouse strong feelings in people. On the other hand, the choice of relatively unemotional or, as I call them, cold words, can reduce strong feelings. When you hear that an ex-convict has just purchased a home next door to you, the word itself can have a strong negative effect on you. The substitution of a word such as non-conformist for ex-convict might lesson your apprehension level.

The clever propagandist chooses his or her words carefully hoping to persuade people to think a certain way. Two examples of how hot and cold words could be selected follows:

Example a:

> Several young boys are dead and you, as the defense attorney for the alleged perpetrators of the crime, want to cool down the jury and reduce any strong feelings they might already have. On the other side is the prosecuting attorney who really wants a conviction of the alleged felons and wants to increase the emotional intensity of the jurors. A hot and cold mixed word list follows:

killed
murdered
butchered
They massacred the boys.
executed
liquidated
terminated
martyred
have slain
slaughtered

You can make your own choice as to which words are hot or cold.

Example b:

> In this case a witness for the prosecution has been caught telling a lie to the jury. The prosecuting attorney wants to defend the witness while the defense attorney wants to do just the opposite. They each must choose words appropriate to their goals.

told an outright lie
told a falsehood
told a story
told a fib
told an untruth
made an unwarranted assertion
told a nursery tale
trumped up a story
told a white lie
made an unfounded declaration
related a false statement

He or she   made an unwarranted assertion   to the jury

Once again, you choose which words or hot or cold.

Instead of offensive words a speaker or writer can choose to use euphemisms, words that are less offensive.

Examples:

Offensive Terms	Euphemisms
Homeless	residentially challenged
Mortuary room	slumber room
Poor student	educationally challenged
Slums	poor environments
Blast the enemy	pacify the enemy
Toilet	restroom
Sex show	adult entertainment
12,000,000 killings	final solution
toilet paper	bathroom tissue

kill the dog	put the dog to sleep
fired	selected out
naughty lawbreaker	severe norm violator
false teeth	dentures
breast meat	white mean

You get the idea! The following two passages will show how euphemisms can put a different slant on a story.

EUPHEMISTIC PASSAGE

Wally was a severe norm violator who lived in a poor environment. As a residentially challenged youth he spent much time at adult entertainment centers. When he was arrested for liberating women's purses, he used many expletives and made a pre-emptive strike against a police person. Even though he as educationally challenged, he vowed that given a chance he would become a tonsorial artist.

TRANSLATION

Wally was a naughty little lawbreaker who lived in a slum. As a homeless youth he spent much time at sex show places. When he was arrested for stealing women's purses, he swore and made a sneak attack on a policeperson. Even though he was a poor student, he vowed that given a chance he would become a barber.

LOOK TO THE FUTURE AND BE OPTIMISTIC

Propagandists can take advantage of people's desire to picture the future as being bright and prosperous. Words and phrases such as innovation, progress, advancement, improvement, high technology, ever upward and onward, reaching the stars, problem solving, high hopes, the bright world of tomorrow, etc. can form a positive attitude in the minds of many.

This technique can work best if the propagandist isn't overly optimistic. A few obstacles should be included in the portrayal of a rosy future.

LET ALTRUISM REIGN

Altruism is concern for the welfare of others as opposed to egoism and selfishness. Many Americans have always thought they were a generous and magnanimous people. They try to help others whenever disasters such as earthquakes, fierce storms, great fires and floods occur.

Telling the audience how generous and caring they are builds up their self-esteem and helps get the message across.

COMBINE FEAR & HOPE

When people are scared they look for safety and security. Propagandists often scare a crowd and then offer hope. The hope usually offered policy or agenda item in the propagandist's message.

PLAY THE EGO CARD

Few of us can resist a propagandist's message that makes us feel important and builds up our ego. Adolf Hitler and his Nazi propagandists told the German people that they were a superior people. Many Germans seem to have bought into the idea with disastrous results.

GO FROM COLD TO MODERATE AND THEN TO HOT

Example: Adolf Hitler was a master of this technique. He would start out speaking slowly and softly and as time passed, he would elevate the emotional intensity of his voice in stages. At the end of his speech the audience would release a tornado of clapping, whistling and shouts of approval.

TURN YOUR OPPONENT INTO A MEMBER OF SOCIETY/S ELITE GROUP

This is the opposite of the " plain folks : technique. The politician running for office will pain his or her opponent as a member of an elite group that is out of touch with the needs of the electorate., will not be a competent fighter for our interests.

SECTION 4 – TECHNIQUES THAT INVOLVE FALSEHOOD OR TRICKERY

QUOTING OUT OF CONTEXT

This technique distorts the meaning of what a person has said about someone or something. The propagandist selects a few words to omit from a given text so as to distort the original meaning. Let's say that the book *Hot Cargo* has been reviewed in a newspaper. The review read "*Hot Cargo* is the best example of an amateurish film released this year." A later advertisement for the film, appropriately altered by the propagandist reads, "*Hot Cargo* is the best...film released this year." When most people see three dots in a sentence, they seldom check out the original sentence to locate omitted words. It helps to e cautious about accepting messages with three dots as completely factual.

USE OF NUMBERS TO IMPRESS

Numbers seem to impress many people. In my state of California as the loot prize figures climb, the sale of tickets increases. Lower dividend figures often impress stockholders in a negative way. Population growth used to be the pride of cities, states and nations as if numbers alone affirmed the greatness of a place.

Some corporations brag about the number of items sold to validate what they manufacture. Prosecuting attorneys of alleged criminals like to mention the number of previous convictions of the accused. The uses of numbers can present a false impression of having the facts and being scientific about the points you are trying to make.

FALSE DILEMMA

A dilemma is a situation that requires one to choose between two equally balanced alternatives. What makes a dilemma false is when only two choices are presented to a person or group, though in fact there are several or many possible choices. A person trying to persuade others knows full well the range of choices but wants to distract the listener by offering seemingly restricted choices.

This technique is illustrated by a political slogan from Denmark in 1935. The slogan "Stauning Eller Kaos" (Stauning Or Chaos) was taken from an election poster of the period and presented the voter with only two choices.

This false dilemma was not confined to Denmark, but seemed to be a common strategy for dictators throughout the world of the 1930s. You'll see it used today.

USING A MINOR POINT TO DISCREDIT A PERSON, PLACE OR THING

This technique tries to make a mountain out of a molehill. In debating, speakers may try desperately to disprove a minor point or seize upon a small matter to discredit their opponent. An automobile salesperson may bring up one small weakness in a competitor's car, such as a lack of leather covered seats, to discredit the whole vehicle.

Using this technique requires caution. If the small point the propagandist brings to light seems like nit-picking, the audience might discredit him or her!

LEADING QUESTION

A leading question is one that, no matter how it is answered, will incriminate the one who answers. A lawyer I once knew said that, in court, you can win a case through "clever" questioning. Never ask a question that doesn't get the answer you want. Examples of leading questions are as follows:

> Have you stopped beating your wife?
> Did you stop your habit of substance abuse?
> Have you stopped committing acts of treason?

SEEK SIMPLE ANSWERS

Demanding a simple answer is a device used by advertisers, politicians and lawyers. For example, a person might hear this question in a television commercial of an automobile company, "Do you ant to see the world's best sedan today?" The advertiser wants a quick affirmative reaction from the viewer. The advertiser does not want a person to research the qualities of the car in a consumer magazine to seek out an evaluation before coming to the showroom.

A politician, after discussing a few examples of outrageous crimes in his or her district might ask the audience, "Do you want to put a stop to crime?" Easier said then done, but he or she hopes to develop an image of being tough on crime issues.

A lawyer for a union of factory workers might well ask a jury, "Do we want to stop all immigration to the United States? I say Yes!, what do you say?" This is a simplistic appeal to a thorny and complex question which needs extensive discussion and examination. The lawyer wants a quick response from the jury and hopefully a positive one for his point of view.

EXAGGERATION OF CONSEQUENCES

Exaggerating the consequence that may follow from the acceptance of someone or something isn't liked, or the rejection of someone or something that is liked is a common debate tactic.

One candidate for public office might claim that if his or her opponent is elected taxes would increase, the budget would e in a shambles and corruption would invade every agency of the government.

An advocate of slow or no growth in a community might react to a proposal from a developer to build new housing by making exaggerations. He or she might say that if new housing is built schools will be so crowded that students will forfeit their education, roads will become parking lots and the environmental damage done by the project will be irreparable.

DOUBLE TALK

Double talk is meaningless speech. It can consist of nonsense words or misplaced words within intelligible speech, or it can simply be contradictory statements.

Some propagandists say two things at once in a contradiction. A hypothetical dictator might say that he or she will end a war but he or she will not just stand around and see his or her friends overrun. The implication here is the dictator will actually remain at war.

A governor of a state might give a speech in which he or she encourages more state support for the state's system of higher education. In the same speech the governor might call for cutting college budgets in order to give tax cuts to the state's taxpayers. All this represents an attempt to try to please two sections of the electorate. Sometimes this kind of double talk fails to please either party.

MANIPULATING NUMBERS

This technique uses numbers to deceive. There are many forms of manipulation and I've selected a few to examine.

Countries with low productivity can deceive by showing the percentage of growth in the production of a selected item rather than present the actual number of an item that was produced.

Telephones Produced

	1998	1999	% of Increase
Nation A	1	2	100%
Nation B	100,000	125,000	25%

This ploy skips the numbers and leads a person into looking at the percentage figures only.

When a person hears a commercial that states that 4 out of 5 doctors do something or use something such as take our insurance or drink a popular beverage, the intent is often to deceive. The advertisers only have to find 4 doctors who use a product or service and 1 who doesn't. Listeners or viewers are supposed to think that thousands of doctors were asked to respond to a survey.

In mathematics there are three types of average, the mean, the mode and the median. The mean is the sum of a group of quantities divided by the number of quantities. For example, the mean average of 6, 8, 12, 14, and 20 is 12 or 60 divided by 5. The mode average is the number that occurs most frequently in a group. The median average is a number that divides a group in half according to size.

Let's pretend to be a real estate salesperson examining a group of homes for sale in a hypothetical community. I'll give the number of homes followed by the asking price. One home for $1,000,000, six homes for $350,000 each, twenty homes for $300,000 each, nine homes for $250,000 each, three homes for $200,000 each, two homes for $150,000 each, six homes for $125,000 each, five homes for $95,000 each and eleven homes for 85,000 each represents the current available housing stock.

In this group of homes the mean average selling price is $469,000, the mode average is $300,000 and the median average is $250,000.

If the realtor had a wealthy client with repulsive personality traits that might cause difficulties within the community, the realtor could present that client with the median average price of homes. The realtor might suggest the client look at a more upscale neighborhood. On the other hand, if the realtor has a relatively poor buyer who wouldn't fit well into the community, the realtor could mention the mean average price which might discourage the client's search for a home in that locale. This is a sophisticated way of persuading people through the manipulation of numbers.

BIG LIE

Big lies are sometimes referred to as being factoids. Factoids are assertions of fact with no evidence to support them. Adolf Hitler used the big lie technique. The idea is that if a lie is big enough, people will tend to think there must be some truth in it. Hitler falsely told the German people that Polish forces had assaulted German army units in an unprovoked attack. Many Germans asked, "Why doesn't Adolf Hitler do something about this?" He did and World War II began.

The big lie was sued a lot before Hitler's rise to power. In World War I the British spread the word that the Germans were cutting off the hands of Belgian children. This was not true.

PLACEMENT OF EMPHASIS

A positive or negative spin can be put on most things. It all depends on what is to be emphasized.

A person might take pride in the fact that say 85% of American homes have indoor plumbing. A detractor of America could stress the fact that 15% of American homes do not have indoor plumbing.

Perhaps a teacher gives his or her class a 100 question examination. A well-liked student might be praised for getting 84 correct answers. A disliked student might be told that he or she answered 16 questions incorrectly.

This technique works fairly well because the facts aren't altered on any topic but puts a spin on things.

USE INNUENDO

An innuendo is implying an accusation without risking refutation by actually saying it. If a person were to hear this statement, "The captain was sober today!" it implies that he's usually drunk. If the propagandist wants to throw a sugar-covered dart at someone or something, then innuendo is effective.

Another slant on this technique is for the propagandist to say he or she isn't saying something and then goes ahead and says it. Some sample statements are, "I'm not saying you're fat but you could lose some weight." And "I'm not calling you a liar, but you should tell the truth."

APPEAL TO IGNORANCE

The principle of this technique is that if something can't be proven it is not so, then it is so. It used to be difficult to prove that cigarettes were bad for a person's health. Court cases against tobacco companies used to be consistently lost. The tobacco companies were always saying that smoking didn't constitute a health problem, and nobody could prove them wrong.

During World War II, Japanese-Americans were rounded up and place din internment camps. If they couldn't prove that they were not spying for Japan, many government officials considered that, in fact, they were spying. In the atmosphere of hate in 1942 too few Americans were willing to take a chance on the loyalty of Japanese-Americans.

A recent example of this technique would be illustrated by the controversy about the influence of violent scenes in motion pictures and on television. The idea is that if you can't prove that violence on television and in the motion pictures makes viewers violent, then these media programs don't make people violent.

CARD STACKING

Only listing the good, or bad, features of a person, place or thing is card stacking. This is really a way of telling a lie by telling the truth, but not the whole truth.

For example an automobile salesperson can distort the truth in order to make a sale.

Characteristics of a Hypothetical Automobile

Good body construction, engine subject to breakdown, inferior radiator, *good carburetor*, poor electrical wiring, *large and convenient back luggage trunk*, poor instrumentation, *excellent brakes*, poor ignition, *comfortable seats*, low quality interior lighting, poor mileage, *excellent sun roof*.

A person can be sure that a potential customer will be presented with all the underlined characteristics of the car.

Commercials often contain this card stacking technique, but you'll find it used by almost every propagandist.

STRESS HIGH MORAL PRINCIPLES

This technique claims that high moral principles (a vague term) characterize the people, ideas or things the propagandist supports. E.G., "My support of Dick Smith for governor is based on his strict adherence to the high moral principles so beautifully expressed by our founding fathers." Many people like to think they are moral and uphold the values dominant in their communities

FALSE URGENCY

Doctors often tell their patients not to rush about so much, but advertisers seem deaf to such advice. A person constantly hears commercials calling for customers to rush down to the store before all items are sold out. If the customers blindly obeyed all of these appeals they'd die from cardiac arrest. People are made to fear that they'll be left out in the cold on bargain sales (greed rears its head again).

PRAISE ONE THING THE OPPONENT HAS DONE. THEN ON TO THE ATTACK

The propagandist can praise one small thing either said or done by his or her opponent and thereby appear to be fair-minded and rather magnanimous. The propagandist also gives the appearance of avoiding the descent into mud slinging. After his or her initial good will gesture or concession, the opposition will be picked apart.

MAKING A MINOR CONFESSION AND SAYING THAT NOW YOU'VE SEEN THE LIGHT

In a speech a propagandist could announce that he or she thought like the opponent, but now sees things differently. This should make the opposition appear to be somewhat backward and reluctant to change his or her position in the light of new evidence. If things go well, the propagandist could come off as a reasonable person who is willing to change after a careful examination of a problem or issue.

SET UP A STRAW MAN

A straw man is a fabricated person, object or matter (issue) used as a purposely weak adversary in a debate.

If a political propagandist is opposed to illegal immigration into the United States, he or she can fabricate a stereotypical illegal immigrant with outlandish and exaggerated characteristics. The fabricated individual will possess an astonishing number of bad tendencies such as criminal behavior (an illegal entry into the United States for example), an inability to read, write or speak English, a willingness to take jobs away from legal immigrants, an eager consumer of welfare funds, etc. This hypothetical straw man would be easy to attack in a debate on the rights of illegal immigrants.

A debate on the importance of greater funding for NASA would lend itself to the use of the straw man technique by propagandists opposed to the space agency. The International Space Station project would become the straw man in the debate. It can be called a waste of our national resources, an unending costly experiment, a drain on other science projects and a publicity stunt for NASA. The fact that there is some opposition to the project makes it relatively difficult to defend as opposed to other NASA projects.

The matter of bilingual education can be argued using the straw man approach. Those opposed to bilingual education can claim that it hinders the learning of English by non-English speaking newcomers to America. The young immigrants will not get good jobs because of their poor English skills. Also, they won't be able to fully participate in the political process of their newly adopted nation. It could be pointed out that bilingual education will produce a flood of future welfare recipients. Obviously the propagandist has made the matter of bilingual education into a monstrous calamity.

The essence of the straw man technique is to exaggerate and/or distort the opponent's argument in order to make it seem illogical or unreasonable.

TELLING THEM YOU WERE GOING TO LIE, BUT COULDN'T DO IT

The propagandist must exercise caution trying this one. It helps if he or she has some acting ability. If done well, the audience might be better disposed to accept the message. People like speakers who at least give the appearance of leveling with them.

For example, a hypothetical mayoral candidate might tell an assembled crowd something like this: "I was going to tell you how great our city is and that it is a role model for other cities in our state. But I can't bring myself to lie to you. You're an intelligent citizenry and both you and I know that this city is in deep trouble. Working together we can turn things around."

BUILD A "POTEMKIN VILLAGE"

Alexandrovich Gregory Potemkin (1739 – 1791) was a Russian administrator serving Empress Catherine the Great. One of his pet projects was the colonization of the Ukraine. He vastly underestimated the cost of the venture and the project was quite unfinished when Catherine took a tour of the Ukraine.

Potemkin tried to cover up the lack of progress and hide it from the eyes of Empress Catherine. There developed an apocryphal tale of Potemkin erecting artificial villages, like Hollywood stage sets, to be seen by the Empress in passing.

"Potemkin Villages" came to denote any pretentious façade designed to cover up a shabby or undesirable condition. If the propagandist needs to cover up something, this technique may work. "Potemkin Villages" have been built at many times and in many places.

In the pre-Civil War American South, southern life was generally portrayed as being quite wonderful. Plantations were shown to be all but a paradise for slaves. Illustrations showed white washed and curtained slave quarters with men playing banjoes and children happily playing under magnolia trees. This fiction was far from the truth as seen in recollections of ex-slaves that have been recorded.

Another example of building a "Potemkin Village" comes from the 1940s. The Nazis built a concentration camp at Theresienstadt in what is now the Czech Republic. It opened in 1941 and closed in 1945 with the allied victory in World War II. The camp, 40 miles from Prague, was built like a little town. It had a library, a zoo, a symphony orchestra, art classes and workshops and a good cafeteria.

Theresienstadt was periodically scrubbed up to impress visiting Red Cross workers. Nazi films portrayed the camp as a paradise for the inmates who were something of an elite group of prisoners in Nazi thinking. Decorated German Jewish soldiers of World War I, Danish Jews and wealthy Jews who paid to avoid being sent to Auschwitz, the most feared death camp, were counted as being lucky. Eventually luck ran out for many prisoners at Theresienstadt as Germany began to lose the war. Disease and malnutrition took their toll.

Hypothetically, a propagandist for a president seeking reelection might draft a speech showing an America that is great, strong, rich and beautiful. The fact that the portrayal is unreal, a "Potemkin Village" probably wouldn't bother him or her at all.

MAKE THE IDEAS BEING SUPPORTED OR OPPOSED SEEM TO BE FOREGONE CONCLUSIONS

If a propagandist supports a particular presidential candidate, then he or she can speak as though that person is all but in the White House already. A display of confidence (perhaps overconfidence) often can sway public opinion in support of the propagandist's choice. Caution: It's true to say that many people supporting other candidates may lose heart feeling that there is no hope for their choices and not go to the polls to cast their votes. It's equally true to say that many others who support the propagandist's choice may not vote because they become overconfident about the outcome of the election and feel that their votes are not necessary.

In a debate, if a person talks as though his or her opponent's position is wrong beyond question, these words may work to win support for his or her side of a question. We can spot similar demonstrations of confidence in court struggles where contending lawyers clash.

DEFINE TERMS TO SUIT GOALS

Defining terms the way the propagandist wishes can eliminate things he or she opposes or supports.

Examples:

If a propagandist rates computers higher than books, he or she can push books to the back burner by defining a library as a repository of electronic information. A budget proposal from the propagandist will certainly favor computers over books.

An advocate for a candidate for high public office can define the word "good" to favor his or her choice. As part of a definition of "good" in what makes a "good candidate ", the advocate might include military service. This definition might well exclude from consideration any other candidates who lack a record of military service to the nation.

BAIT & SWITCH

Some businesses entice customers to buy their goods and/or services by advertising a bargain price. Then the customer is told , " Sorry but we're all sold out. But wait, we do have some great substitutes at a slightly higher price." If this happens to you and you purchas something then you have most likely become a victim of the bait and switch technique.

CREATE A NEGATIVE VIEW OF AN OPPONENT WITHOUT MAKING DIRECT ACCUSATIONS

Example: A political campaign speech begins with these questions? " Would it bother you if you found out that my opponent lied about his voting record? ; Would it bother you if you found out that my opponent was a spouse abuser?

SECTION 5-TECHNIQUES THAT PLAY ON HUMAN BEHAVIORAL TENDENCIES

APPEAL TO AUTHORITY

Many people don't like being self-directed. Making decisions and thinking for themselves make some people fearful and/or nervous. When someone tells them what to think or do it is quite relaxing. They just do what they're told and abdicate any responsibility for their actions.

In an appeal to authority the propagandist simply tells people what to do or think. Examples would be statements that proclaim, "Drink Milk" or "Join the Army" or "Support Your Party." With this technique the propagandist doesn't have to provide reasons or explanations. People are just supposed to do what they are told.

REPETITION

Even the thickest skull can be penetrated by a message if it is repeated often enough. It would be wise for the propagandist to repeat the message with some variation. The German dictator, Adolf Hitler, wrote, "The intelligence of the masses is small. Their forgetfulness is great. They must be told the same thing a thousand times." It would appear that many advertisers today agree with him.

During my high school days, a friend of mine rejected the idea that he should study and get good grades. In a class on American government, he refused to take any notes on the teacher's lectures. Instead he read newspapers and magazines, quietly at the back of the class. He made no troubles so the teacher never took action against his lack of cooperation.

The teacher's lectures on the Constitution stressed constant repetition. Statements such as "Each state has two senators.", "Supreme Court justices serve life terms.", etc., were repeated frequently. On a Constitution test of multiple choice questions my friend got an A grade. The repeated information had been imbedded in his brain. He failed the course but he learned the effectiveness of repetition as a teaching technique. You'll see repetition in most political and advertising campaigns.

USE SLOGANS

The word slogan most likely originated as a battle cry of ancient Scottish or Irish warriors. It is defined as a phrase expressing the aims or nature of an enterprise or organization. The word motto is a synonym for slogan. A slogan can be thought of as an abbreviated idea which, hopefully, will persuade people to think as you want them to think.

One of the most persistent human efforts is for elite groups in any society to try to persuade, brainwash, those members of society lower on the social class structure to think or act in a desired way. What better way to do this than to create a simplified easily remembered statement.

Slogans are not designed to be carefully examined but to be accepted without question. Slogans can be very short or long lived. They can be as short as one word or as long as a brief paragraph. Some are catchy while others are plain and straight forward.

One example of a catchy American slogan comes to us from the mid-nineteenth century. In several cities in America, political parades were held in which the participants were shouting, "Fifty-four forty or fight!" This slogan reflected a goal of President James K. Polk to gain land in the Oregon Country from Great Britain. The Oregon Controversy between the United States and Great Britain was settled by a compromise in 1846 which resulted in the border between British Columbia, Canada and the United States being drawn at the 49th parallel of latitude.

One of the best slogans that I recently noticed in San Francisco, California was crafted to make street crossings safer for pedestrians. The slogan read, "Feeling run down? You will if you cross at the wrong time buster."

BANDWAGON

Most people feel comfortable when what they do is also done by many other people. Like kids jumping on a circus bandwagon, people can be swept away by the enthusiasm of a crowd.

I remember a visit I paid to New Orleans. When it came time to have dinner I walked down a street in the famous French Quarter of the city. I looked into one restaurant and saw that there were uniformed waiters with white linen towels draped over their arms. I could see comfortable chairs, beautifully decorated tables, a fine bar and colorful potted plants. There was only one thing missing – customers! As I glanced further on down the street, I saw a long line of customers outside another restaurant. Where do you think I ate dinner that night? You guessed it! I took my place in the line and felt quite comfortable doing it.

Reportedly, a British journalist fluent in German attended a Nazi rally and found himself giving Adolf Hitler a salute with his outstretched right arm as everyone else was doing. The journalist was shocked by his own behavior for he was certainly no supporter of the Fuehrer.

Supporters of a Democratic presidential candidate might say, "Everyone is going Democrat this year." The same claim might be made by a supporter of the Republicans.

PLAIN FOLKS

This is an appealing technique for politicians, entertainers and spokespersons. If they are regular guys and gals, an average audience appears to like them better. Most people are uncomfortable in the company of very wealthy people, famous personalities or outstanding experts in various fields. Knowing this can work to the benefit of propagandists.

America's presidents, from George Washington, the kid who reportedly chopped down a cherry tree to Abraham Lincoln the rail splitting lawyer and more recently the touch football playing of John F. Kennedy, have demonstrated that they're just regular fellows who act in ways similar to your next door neighbors.

Motion picture magazines and celebrity journals often show the rich and famous of the entertainment world pursuing hobbies, decorating their homes and playing with their children. These activities create a good image in the collective body of fans throughout the world.

Very bright people and outstanding students make many of their fellows nervous. In a history class that I taught in high school, I had an exceptionally outstanding student. He knew all of the answers to the questions given to the class but he seldom raised his hand. In a conversation I had with him, I mentioned his restraint. He volunteered that he didn't want to appear to dominate the class. Later, I found out that he had been elected to be the president of the class. If he had acted as a "know-it-all" I doubt that he would have been so successful in school politics.

TRANSFER

This technique attempts to transfer either good or bad feelings the propagandist might have towards a person, place or thing to another person, place or thing.

If people see you in the company of crooks they tend to think of you as a crook. If, on the other hand, you are seen with high status people, you are usually thought to be of high status as well. It's a form of the old saying, "You are judged by the company you keep."

Advertisers use transfer considerably. A group of young and beautiful men and women at a beach are shown drinking a national brand soft drink, viewers or listeners are supposed to transfer their good feelings they have toward the young people to the soft drink.

Anti-smoking advocates will show cigarette smoking people coughing terribly in images that viewers, it is hoped, will transfer to the act of lighting up cigarettes.

TESTIMONIAL

This technique makes use of popular well known people to support a person, a product or an idea. An expert is seldom used in making a testimonial advertisement. If the propagandist is trying to sell shoes he or she is much better off using a well known basketball star to support the product than a career shoemaker that few people know. Hero worship trumps reason in many ways.

In politics one important job of a political leader is to make speeches in support of his or her fellow party members who are campaigning for office. Later on the leader can collect I.O.Us from those whom he or she gave testimonials to in the hopes of winning re-election.

USING A BIAS

A bias is a preference or inclination that inhibits impartial judgement. A bias can slant in two different directions.

Biases may support, condone or praise certain people, places, ideas or things that are considered to be important and positive among a large group of people in a given society.

On the other hand, biases may feature condemnation or opposition to certain people, places, ideas and things that are considered to be evil, destructive or anti-social by a large group of people in a given society.

If a propagandist wants to make use of a bias in a speech or commercial, he or she will have some work to do. The audience should be investigated to uncover any possible biases that can be used to support or attack the issue being debated. Caution is called for after the biases have been discovered so as not to alienate any important segment of the audience.

Every society has its sacred cows, a person, place, idea or thing that is considered to be so important that few people speak out against them. . In Indian society the cow is traditionally held in such high esteem that is has become sacred. Its importance to the community is beyond question. The Hindus generally feel that all animals have souls, but the cow is the most sacred of all animals. Poor treatment of a cow is considered to be disgraceful behavior and the consumption of beef is avoided by devout Hindus.

One way to identify positive biases, or things many people strongly support, is to look at a few sacred cows in American society.

Some American Sacred Cows:

Economic Sacred Cows:

Private property, capitalism, free enterprise, the right to form business

Political Sacred Cows:

> The presidency, the Supreme Court, the Constitution, tax exemption for places of worship, the flag, national holidays, the two-party system, democracy, the welfare system, the present system of states, the right of immigration into the United States, the legal settlement

of disputes, the national anthem, social security, the Electoral College.

Religious Sacred Cows:

The clergy, the Pope, the cross, the Ten Commandments, Religious holidays, holy places, belief in God, sacred texts

Social Sacred Cows:

Children, weddings, marriage, the right to reproduce, motherhood, the family, doctors, the dead, funerals, burial grounds, mass public education, college education, graduation ceremonies, endangered species, historical buildings, historical statues and symbols, the goodness of rural life, man as the sexual aggressor, man as the decision maker, man as warrior, spectator sports, mobility, the automobile, progress, home ownership, egalitarianism, the right of inheritance, the right to strike, the right to choose your mate, aid to the disabled, paid vacations.

Some of these sacred cows are slowly dying or are being seriously questioned while new ones are emerging and being added to the list.

Every society also has its list of taboos, or negative biases. These are people, places, ideas and things that people oppose or are generally think of as undesirable. Let's look at some of them.

Some Taboos

Economic Taboos:

High places, low demand for goods and services, disparity between high and low salary scales in the workplace, low salaries, depression, recession, stock market crashes, scarcity

Political Taboos:

> High taxes, a police state, union of church and state, poor educational system, poor health care, pollution, slavery

Religious Taboos:

> Favoritism of one religion over another by the government, immoral scenes in the mass media, desecration of sacred objects, seizure of religious properties, demands for non-discriminatory practices against women, gays, etc.

Social Taboos:

> Crime, substance abuse, terrorism, disloyalty, corruption, bribery, too rapid a rate of societal change, spousal abuse, child abuse, abuse of senior citizens, cruelty to animals, juvenile delinquency, suicide, scandals

What has been said about sacred cows can be said about taboos. Some are dying or are being seriously questioned while new ones are emerging.

One example of a politician using a bias from the list of sacred cows would be for him or her to stress the American value of mobility. The politician might be trying to persuade the audience to support a freeway expansion.

One example of using a bias from American's taboo list would be for a propagandist opposed to school reform to select the high tax taboo. People generally have bad feelings when the topic of high taxes is introduced.

The propagandist could stress the great expense that would be incurred by the taxpayers in any serious attempt to bring about educational reform.

CHALLENGE TO THE EGO

Some people need to know they've got what it takes. This challenge to the ego technique was made for them. I remember an appeal from the United States Marine Corps which said something like " you can join the Marines if you're man enough." I'm sure that the Marine Corps hoped many young men would take the bait and join up.

I once tried to use this technique on my son. I said that I didn't think he had the strength to lift up the garbage can from the garage and take it out in front of the house. This ploy only worked once as my son soon got wise to my intentions.

FLATTERY WILL WORK WONDERS

Flattery is something people often say they don't like, but don't you believe it. If flattery isn't overdone, it can prepare an audience to better receive ideas. Flattery can defuse some angry crowds at times.

People like to be thought of as being intelligent. You can tell them they are capable of thinking for themselves and drawing their own conclusions. Of course their conclusions are based on the facts you have given them.

An audience that has been told they are needed and important to the cause will be more likely to support the ideas of the propagandist. Likewise, an audience that has been told of the sympathy that is with them for any sacrifices they have made will often be won over. Most people are hungry for recognition of any suffering they feel they have endured.

Audiences like to feel powerful. People generally like to feel that they are empowered. When they are told they are members of a winning team t hey will feel they are in control of events.

EMPHASIZING CREDENTIALS

Good credentials such as titles, degrees or awards usually impress listeners. A propagandist in speaking on an issue in American history probably would open with something like, "Since receiving my doctorate in history, I've studied American political affairs exhaustively. And I believe that...."

TELL THEM IT'S CONFIDENTIAL

In this technique a propagandist says what he or she is about to tell the audience is strictly confidential and privileged information. Since people generally like to think that they are "in the know" and members of the "in crowd" they are likely to accept whatever they are told. The propagandist leaks a small item from a news story or relates a new finding, hoping to win approval and support from an audience.

STIMULATE CURIOSITY

Whenever a propagandist can stimulate people to be curious, he or she will do it. Commercials in the mass media often include invitations to potential customers to come on down to the store and see the bargains, products or services for themselves. There is a human tendency to investigate things. Automobile dealers often encourage customers to take a test drive in any one of the new cars on the showroom floor. Publicists for cities and states often ask people to send for free brochures that loaded with colorful and interesting pictures that will hopefully attract visitors.

In a debate, a propagandist might tell his or her audience, "Would you really like to know what's behind my opponent's proposal?" The audience should be expected to show a little more interest that usual in what they're being told.

One of the debaters might suggest to the members of the audience the questions they should ask of the opponent. The opponent will then feel obligated to answer those questions. The propagandist should be sure that the questions suggested center on the weakest parts of the opposition's case.

This could put the opponent on the spot.

STRUCTURED RESPONSE

In this technique the propagandist tries to get people to respond to his or her questions with a continual stream of like answers, either positive or negative, depending on how the propagandist wants to influence the audience. The questions should be such that most people would respond in the same way. After several questions are asked the propagandist slips in the question he or she is really interested in being answered in a certain way. The propagandist hopes that habit will kick into play and that the crowd will come up with the response he or she wants.

Example:

If a politician was against gun control, he or she might ask a series of questions as follows:

> Speaker: "Do you want government censorship?
> Audience: "No!"

> Speaker: "Do you want high taxes?"
> Audience: "No!"

> Speaker: "Do you want to live in a police state?"
> Audience: "No!"

> Speaker: "Do you want big government to keep on growing?"
> Audience: "No!"

> Speaker: "Do you want your sons and daughters to be sent off to war?"
> Audience: "No!"

> Speaker: "Do you want government gun control?"
> Audience: "No!"

IMITATE, MIMIC OR MOCK THE OPPONENT

If a propagandist attempts to put down the opposition using this technique, he or she better have some talent in the performing arts. Apparently, President Harry S. Truman did. On the eve of the presidential election of 1948, H.V. Kaltenborn, a famous radio announcer, stood by his view that Thomas E. Dewey, the Republican candidate, would defeat Truman. Kaltenborn expected a strong last minute flood of rural

Republican voters would enable Dewey to pull ahead of Truman and win the White House.

The victorious Harry Truman showed no mercy to H.V. Kaltenborn. Truman publicly mocked the nation's renowned commentator, by imitating the man's facial expressions, gestures and speech to restate Kaltenborn's incorrect projection of the election results.

AD POPULUM

This is a device that relies in featuring whatever is current, well known or popular at the time. Simply put this technique focuses on what the propagandist thinks his or her audience wants to hear and is currently interested or concerned about.

In my classrooms at the turn of the 21st century, I find that most students place the Vietnam War in the category of ancient history. References to that war in any school debate would fall on deaf ears.

To effectively persuade an audience the propagandist must make his or her points relevant to the times.

ACTION INVOLVEMENT

If the propagandist has a chance, he or she will enlist the members of the audience in taking some action for a cause. A situation can be created in which people bond with the speaker and his or her aims. In this technique the propagandist will call on people to write letters, make telephone calls, ring doorbells, talk to friends, make financial contributions, distribute flyers and do anything to get them personally involved. The more people do for a cause, the more they'll likely support it.

PRESENT UTOPIAN OR DYSTOPIAN FANTASIES

A utopia literally means "no place", but generally is taken to mean an imaginary perfect society. A utopian view can paint a wonderful picture of the future in which all of our social, political, economic and environmental problems are solved.

Propagandists who project utopian concepts cater to a tendency of many people to seek perfection. We all want good outcomes from our endeavors. Many political and religious leaders have projected what they thought were perfect social orders. Hitler's Thousand Year Reich, Stalin's worker's paradise, Mussolini's forecast of the new Roman Empire, Savonarola's heavenly Florence, Napoleon's new Europe, Brigham Young's new zion in Utah – all were utopian visions.

Any politician who can stimulate his or her people to dream of a great, prosperous and problem free future is using the utopian technique on them. If a propagandist wants to research some utopian constructions of the past, he or she might examine a few of the following utopian authors and their works:

Andreae, J.V. *Christianopolis*
Bacon, Francis *The New Atlantis*
Bellamy, Ed *Looking Backward*
Brown, J.M. *Limanora*
Burton, Robert *An Utopia of Mine Own*
Butler, Samuel *Erewhon*
Cabet, Etienne *Voyage en Icarie*
Campanella, Tommasco *City of the Sun*
Chavannes, Albert *The Future Commonwealth*
Chauncey, Thomas *The Crystal Button*
Ellis, G. A. *New Britain*
Donnelly, Ignatius *Caesar's Column*
Harrington, James *Oceana*
Hertzka, Dr. Theodor *Freeland*
Huxley, Aldous *Brave New World*
Lao-tzu *II Ching*
Macrie, John *The Diothas*
More, Sir Thomas *Utopia*
Plato *The Republic*
Skinner, B.F. *Waldon Two*
Stanley, William *The Case of the Fox*
Tarde, Gabriel *Underground Man*
Wells, H.G. *A Modern Utopia*

A dystopia is the worst imaginable society. If a person is in, let's say, a race for the presidency, he or she might try to portray a dystopia. The trick is to show how terrible the nation will be if the opponent wins the election.

If the propagandist wants to explore some dystopias, he or she might examine the following authors and their works:

Hall, Joseph *The Discovery of a New World*
Orwell, George *1984*

SCARCITY SELLS

Few things attract human interest as the perception of scarcity. Scarce items usually have high value and corporate advertising makes good use of this. A real estate developer can hardly resist saying how few homes are left in his or her development.

A selective college or university seems to attract students to it. The possession or attainment of something scarce often means high prestige for the person who won the race.

SECTION 6-TECHNIQUES OF STYLE

SHOCK 'EM

A propagandist will use the shock treatment to catch his or her audience's attention. The propagandist will make a rather outrageous, exaggerated or shocking statement as an attention getter. There is a price to pay for using this technique. The propagandist must have the necessary supporting data and sound reasons to back up any shocking opening remark.

I've listed a few examples of hypothetical shocking statements that might be made by partisans of some selected issues:

An Environmentalist: "The human race might not see the turn of the next century."

An Educational Reformer: "America's public schools are pretty good – for a third world nation!"

A Dietitian : "You may be killing your children."

An Opponent of Anti-ballistic missile systems: We're more likely to die from a terrorist bombing than from a missile launched from a rogue nation."

A Sociologist with a Bias Against Extreme Social Stratification: "Karl Marx might have been right. The rich are getting richer and the poor are getting poorer."

A Scientist Concerned About Global Warming: "Pretty soon we'll have to visit our coastal cities from a sight seeing submarine."

An Ultra-feminist: "Who are the most dangerous people in the world? They're fairly easy to spot for they usually wear pants!"

A Doctor Pitted against Health Insurance Companies: "Could we win a war if our generals had to get permission to go ahead with each planned battlefield maneuver? Well doctors are facing similar circumstances today!"

One outstanding example of the shock'em technique was provided by the antics of the evangelist Aimee Semple Mc Pherson. In the late 1920s, her illustrated sermons became famous. After receiving a traffic ticket for speeding she had an idea for a sermon. One day she called out to her congregation, "Stop! You're under arrest!" Sister Aimee, as she was called, appeared on her temple platform in a police uniform, standing by a motorcycle with the sound of police siren's echoing throughout the Temple. She challenged her people to stop before they sped into hell.*

*Blumhofer, Edith *Aimee Semple McPherson: Everybody's Sister* William B. Eerdmans Publishing Co. Grand Rapids, Michigan 1993, pg. 261.

THE SHOTGUN APPROACH

With this technique the propagandist throws at the audience every supporting idea for his or her cause that can be thought up. The hope is that at least some of the ideas will be accepted. The more varied and heterogeneous the audience is, the better the chances to get ideas across. If the propagandist is scared to base his or her case on just one main point, this approach is a wise one.

EMPHASIZE ONE POINT

With this technique the propagandist selects what he or she feels is the strongest argument supporting the position being taken on a subject. All other supporting arguments are excluded. It can be risky because if the opponent shoots down the propagandist's main idea the contest is over.

Abraham Lincoln debated using this approach. He was seriously opposed to slavery and in his speeches he hammered away at the problem relentlessly. The slave holding states didn't like him one bit but the free states certainly did and elected him to the presidency.

BREAK THE ICE

The propagandist can warm up an audience to better accept the message being delivered by first telling a joke or amusing story. The audience will be more receptive to the message once their tensions are relieved.

Let's say that a speech is being given in New York City. Listeners could be told, "I almost broke my neck looking at the tops of your tall skyscrapers here." (The Propagandist rubs his or her neck a little while making the remark.)

The propagandist will have amassed a collection of jokes and amusing stories appropriate to reach the groups being targeted. I've listed some topics used to break the ice.

alliteration, bathos, pathos, burlesqsue, caricature, conundrums, crazy acronyms, daffy definitions, irony, epigrams, hyperbole, limericks, oxymora, parody, puns, ridicule, sarcasm, sardonic remarks, satire, sick humor, synecdoche, understatement

START COLD, GET WARM AND END HOT

I've seen motion pictures of Adolf Hitler making speeches where he used this technique to influence the crowd. He would begin calmly, like an old kindly grandfather, to slowly address his audience. Then he would begin speaking a little faster and louder and with a notable increase in enthusiasm. He would end his speech by screaming at the crowd while gesturing forcibly and using his fists to pound the podium. The crowd seemed to have accompanied the Fuehrer in his mood swings and went wild with cheers and applause.

BUILDING THE MESSAGE AROUND A PROVERB

A proverb is a short, pithy saying that expresses a well known truth or fact in the minds of many people.

A propagandist might begin his or her speech or article with a proverb. It could be selected so as to lend support to the message being delivered. After stating the proverb, the propagandist would build a case by offering several arguments based on the proverb.

Examples of Selected Proverbs and Their Possible Uses:

Proverb: Ambition destroys its possessor.
Possible Use: Attacking a strong opponent in a race for political office.

Proverb: Do good, and not ask for whom.
Possible Use: Making a pitch for charitable donations.

Proverb: How far that little candle throws his beams!
Possible Use: An appeal for people to do one small deed for a cause.

Proverb: Only the educated are free.
Possible Use: A campaign for increased aid to education.

Proverb: A good husband makes a good wife. A good wife makes a good husband.
Possible Use: Making a plea for gender equality.

Proverb: Our fears always outnumber our dangers.
Possible Use: A propaganda appeal in support of a risky project.

Proverb: A little too late is much too late.
Possible Use: To criticize a town council's promised programs that were never completed.

Proverb: When money speaks, truth keeps silent.
Possible Use: An attack on powerful pressure groups in a state or national capital.

Proverb: Never open the door to a little vice lest a great one enter with it.
Possible Use: Someone speaking out against the legalization of marijuana.

USING GESTURES AND PROPS

Humans, perhaps more than other animals, are able to show a great variety of facial expressions and body language to display emotional states and desires.

If you've ever seen many speeches, especially those given by political and religious personalities, you've undoubtedly witnessed many uses of human body parts to persuade. Who hasn't seen finger-pointing, clenched fists, chest and podium pounding, thumbs either up or down, arms akimbo and other shows of facial expression and body language?

In the 19th century, gestures in speech functioned as a code for various states of feeling projected by a speaker. In the 20th century, gesture language went out of vogue but is still with us in a less complicated form. The clever propagandist will often practice expressions of the face and body attempting to win the response he or she wants from the audience.

Props are stage properties used in show business. The art of propaganda resembles dramatic art in some ways. Increasingly, public opinion is shaped by more than words alone. Image making is the rage today and props are necessary to this enterprise. Some often seen props are listed as follows:

> insignias: flags, medals, ribbons, hats, uniforms, logos, badges of authority, etc.

> large picture backdrops

> books: used as a backdrop to make the speaker seem scholarly and wise

> charts and graphs

> music

> sound effects

> mood lighting

> video screens tied to the internet

MAKING A STATEMENT THAT DOESN'T FACE REBUTTAL

In a typical traditional form of debate, there are usually two speakers on each side of a proposition. Two speakers are for the proposition (the affirmative side) and two speakers are against the proposition (the negative side).

Each speaker delivers both a constructive speech and a rebuttal speech. A constructive speech presents facts and evidence for or against a proposition, while a rebuttal speech answers the arguments and evidence of the opposing speakers.

In this traditional debate form the speaking order is:

Constructive speeches (eight minutes each)
1. First affirmative
2. First negative
3. Second affirmative
4. Second negative

Rebuttal speeches (four minutes each)
1. First negative
2. First affirmative
3. Second negative
4. Second affirmative

The rebuttal speech of the second affirmative provides the speaker an opportunity to make a strong statement, perhaps a catchy slogan, which will not leave time for any rebuttal.

MAKING A PRE-EMPTIVE STRIKE

A propagandist attacks his or her opposition on the point that is central to their case before they the opposition opens their mouths. In this technique the first affirmative debater challenges or answers the opposition's strongest argument. In this way it's possible to defuse the thrust of the opponent's attack.

There is danger in doing this maneuver. If the debater makes a miscalculation about his or her opponent's chief argument it could mean trouble.

SECTION 7-TECHNIQUES OF REASON AND COMMON SENSE

USING THE SOCRATIC METHOD

Socrates (469 B.C.-399 B.C.) is the famous Greek philosopher who developed what is now called the Socratic Method.

This technique works well with two or a few people in a philosophical conversation. It is assumed the terms being used in the discussion are well understood and have clear definitions accepted by all the participants. As the discussion progresses, it becomes apparent, through careful questioning, that the definitions of terms differed or had minor flaws. It would then become apparent that true knowledge of an issue or problem being discussed was inadequate to reach a sound conclusion. As more time passes, the definitions of terms would improve becoming more universal and applicable to all examples.

No satisfactory conclusion might be reached, but the goal of finding true and universal definitions would be furthered.

In the Socratic Method, ignorance must be acknowledged, to do otherwise is to take a "know-it-all position.

Propagandists can use the Socratic way of arguing with someone who bring sup ideas such as there should be a drug free America, family values must be upheld, Caucasians are a superior race or males should dominate females. In each of these statements, definitions would be carefully examined through extensive questioning. The discussion leader could start by asking questions such as "What is a drug?", "What are family values?," "What is a Caucasian?", "What does it mean to be superior?" "What is a male and a female?" and "What does it mean to dominate?"

This technique is designed to break apart vague definitions used by opponents. If the propagandist is lucky, he or she may put the opposition on the ropes if they haven't done their homework on the terms they use. The opponents may try several countermeasures. One might be to use a non-sequitur and another might be to answer the question with another question. The skilled propagandist always tries to prepare for his or her opponent's countermeasures.

USE METAPHORS AND SIMILES

The use of figures of speech helps to leave main ideas in the minds of an audience. Of all the figures of speech used by propagandists, I have noticed that metaphors and similes seem to head the list.

A metaphor is a figure of speech in which a term is transferred from the object it ordinarily designates to an object it may designate only by implicit comparison or analogy.

Examples:

Metaphors	Literal Meanings
Evening of life	last years
Slime bucket with legs	a truly terrible person
A watermelon	a fat person
Catcher's mitts	large hands

A simile is a figure of speech in which two essentially unlike things are compared and typically uses the words "like" or "as".

Examples:

That symphony orchestra sounds like a thousand meowing cats all out of tune.

She's as nutty as the topping on a chocolate sundae.

The new dog was running around the yard like a balloon that suddenly lost all of its air.

One good example of the use of similes is the acceptance speech made by George Herbert Walker Bush at the Republican National Convention in New Orleans on August 18, 1988. He said, "We are a nation of communities, of tens and tens of thousands of ethnic, religious, social, business, labor union, neighborhood, regional and other organizations, all of them varied, voluntary and unique...a brilliant diversity spread like stars, like a thousand points of light in a broad and peaceful sky."

TURN A PROBLEM INTO AN OPPORTUNITY

In public speaking the propagandist often has to deal with hecklers and usually is prepared for this kind of situation. When heckling started at a speech being delivered by a prominent candidate for the presidency, he responded "One great thing about our country is that people here have the freedom to speak their minds."

Sample Responses to Hecklers:

> A name-calling heckler: "In words that I learned in the playground, sticks and stones will break my bones but names will never hurt me."

> Accusations of wrong doing: "Let he who is without sin cast the first stone."

> Embarrassing question: "I won't dignify that question with an answer."

> Foul language: "Your dear mother would be ashamed of your behavior tonight!"

> Sarcastic remark: "Hey buddy or lassie, you're sharp as a drill and twice as boring!"

HELP FROM GIANTS OF THE PAST AND PRESENT

A politician raging against his or her opponent who holds high office might quote the famous statement made by Lord Aston, "All power corrupts, and absolute power corrupts absolutely."

A propagandist using quotations can come off as a person who is educated, scholarly and wise when well selected quotations are used appropriately.

TURN A WEAKNESS INTO A STRENGTH

Propagandists who have sinned or done something wrong, claim they've been reborn as a more effective people.

A political party not anticipating a particular problem, say they don't waste time planning for things before they happen, but remain flexible and ready to meet any problem.

A group of students criticized for having mediocre grades, say that being well-rounded and not specialized in academics, has been a blessing. They are better prepared for life outside of the ivory tower.

CHOOSE WORDS WISELY

Propagandists tailor their vocabulary to suit their target audiences. Foreign words and phrases are avoided unless the audience is a group of scholarly folks. If propagandist's choices of words makes them incomprehensible to their listeners, they'll usually lose them.

YES, BUT...

Occasional conspicuous candor can help build a propagandist's long range credibility. Josef Goebbels, Nazi Germany's propaganda chief, practiced candor on the German people. He said yes, we are losing the war, but secret weapons being developed will turn things around. Because of his seeming honesty, many people in Nazi Germany believed him.

When Vice President Richard Nixon traveled to the Soviet Union in July 1959 to open an American exhibit in Moscow, many Russians put the representatives of American on the spot. American attendants were asked some rather tough questions. Russians wanted to know why African Americans were oppressed. It isn't wise for a propagandist to directly contradict his or her audience and the American attendants knew that. Their response was a "Yes, but..." way of handling the question. They acknowledged that it was a serious domestic problem, but that we were trying to make a more just situation. This response, according to observers, seemed to make the Russians more receptive to what we had to say on other issues.

BE SENSATIVE TO GENDER DIFFERENCES IN YOUR AUDIENCE

In a patriarchal such as in the United States, don't create an appeal restricted to males. Half of our people are woman and you should always remember to speak to them if you are a good propagandist.

STUDY CULTURAL ANTHROPOLOGY

It's advisable for a propagandist who lives in a pluralistic society to study the cultures represented in the audience being addressed. Special attention should be given to the values and taboos of each culture you may be encountering.

PLAY THE " I WAS WRONG " CARD

Example: A convert to a re;gion who wants to get the support and acceptance might say this to the congregation: When I was a mindless child, I didn't believe in God. I thought that religion was a waste of time. Now that I've grown up and my mind thinks clearly, I see the light. Halleluhah!

PERSUADE BY EXAMPLE:

A politician running for a high office might say to an audience of his constituents, " I fought for change and reform all of my life. As president of my high school class I fought for student rights. In college, I led a battle against an administration that restricted student rights. As president , I will continue the struggle , with your support, to protect your rights.

EXERCISES FOR SECTION 1

Practice in using the techniques of Section 1:

SIMPLIFICATION

Write a simplified summary of the American Declaration of Independence.

Write an easy to understand explanation of what a customer should look for in purchasing an automobile.

CONCURRENCY

Choose any policy, person, product or thing you *oppose* and try to link it with negative associations (Hint: If you would oppose the use of alcoholic beverages, link that use with a concurrent increase in highway fatalities and violent crimes.)

Choose any policy, person, product or thing you *support* and try to link it with positive associations. (Hint: If you would support NASA, try to link the agency with other fields in which are simultaneously advancing our body of knowledge.)

POST HOC

Choose a politician or policy that you *support* and try to establish a series of positive effects that flowed from the actions of the politician or the enforcement of the policy.

Choose a politician or policy that you *oppose* and try to establish a series of negative effects that flowed from the actions of the politician or the enforcement of the policy.

GENERALIZATION

Use several generalizations in a *negative* descriptive paragraph of any person, place or thing of your choice.

Use several generalizations is a *positive* descriptive paragraph of any person, place or thing of your choice.

FAULTY ANALOGY

Make a claim that going to school is analogous to going to work. Present reasons to support your analogy. In a separate paragraph, show why your analogy is faulty.

Claim that the carrying out of capital punishment by a state government is analogous to the killing of cattle in a slaughterhouse. Present reasons to support your analogy. In a separate paragraph, show why your analogy is faulty.

CONDEMNING THE ORIGIN

Write a xenophobic (fear or hatred of foreigners) article in which you condemn something because of its foreign origin. (Hint: You could condemn the use of high school exit examinations because of a French origin or you could deplore the use of foreign words and expressions in our American language usage.)

FALSE CONVERSION OF PROPOSITIONS

Write a political statement followed by an assertion that does not follow. (Hint: You could say that Republicans and Democrats are truly patriotic Americans and then go on to state that all true Americans are either Republicans or Democrats.)

WHAT IS TRUE OF THE PARTS IS TRUE FOR THE WHOLE

Write a paragraph in support of a politician of your choice claiming that his or her good points are indicative of his or her general character.

THE BLACK AND WHITE FALLACY

Write a paragraph in support of a proposed amendment to the United States Constitution using the black and white fallacy. (Hint: You could claim that those who oppose the removal of the Electoral College system from the Constitution are undemocratic while those who support it are democratic.)

USING AN ILLICIT DEFINITION

Choose any of the following words and write an example of how the definition of the word can be altered, twisted and/or made to be misleading:

Word List: democracy, depression, pornography, sexual harassment. (Hint: Use the word communism to cover all socialist systems of government in the world.)

FALLACY OF BIASED SAMPLING

Choose a subject for polling. Solicit responses to your questions from at least fifteen people of the same sex, approximate age and occupation as you. Tabulate the results. Then ask at least fifteen people of the opposite sex, age and occupation as your own. Tabulate the results. Do you find great differences in your results? Explain.

THE GAMBLER'S FALLACY

Write a paragraph using this fallacy to encourage people to play a lottery game or write a paragraph as if you were a stockbroker in which role you encourage customers to buy a stock plagued by a poor performance record.

THE FALLACY OF INCONSISTENCY

Choose any topic and write about it using inconsistent premises. (Hint: A graduation speaker says that all graduates should go to college or vocational schools to prepare for a career. The speaker then appeals to the girls in the class to get married, have children and stay home to raise them.)

APPEAL TO INAPPROPRIATE AUTHORITY

Write an advertisement using this technique for any product, to support a political candidate, or to advocate a cause or policy of your choice.

SECTION REVIEW PAPER

Write a propaganda paper for a politician, product or cause of your choice in which you use at least three of the techniques from the exercises in section 1. At the end of your paper, write the names of the techniques you have selected to use in your writing.

BUILDING VOCABULARY

Define the following words used in section 1 and use each of them in a sentence.

Word List: logic, concurrency, post hoc, correspondence, proposition, polarized, illicit, invalid

EXERCISES FOR SECTION 2

Practice in using the techniques of Section 2:

USE OF AMBIGUOUS WORDS

Use ambiguous words in writing an appeal to high school students to go to an imaginary or actual college or university. Underline the ambiguous words that you have used in your appeal. (Words such as good, superior, comprehensive, friendly, progressive, innovative, prestigious, high rated, exciting, and multi-cultural are often used in publicity messages for colleges and universities.)

AD HOMINEM

This is your chance to go primitive in letting off steam. Choose any person, place or thing and go on a verbal attack with words as barbed weapons.

BEGGING THE QUESTION

Make three unproven statements, as though they were fact, in support of any person, place or thing of your choice. After this, make three unproven statements, as though they were fact, in opposition to any person, place or thing of your choice.

THE WICKED ALTERNATIVE

Support any person, place or thing of your choice by pointing to its wicked alternative. (Hint: I know Dad has a serious disease but it's better than a coffin.)

NON-SEQUITUR

List any three questions you feel would be a challenge to a person being questioned. Answer each question using the non-sequitur technique. Whatever you do, don't in any way really answer the question, just seem to be answering the question.

ACCUSING THE ACCUSER

Write three accusative statements aimed at an imaginary opponent. Have the imaginary opponent make a counter accusation in response to each accusative statement. *Hint: Older Brother, "You didn't eat your spinach! Younger Brother, "Yeah! You didn't eat your carrots!")

NAME CALLING

Research newspapers, magazines, radio and television broadcasts, the Internet and books looking for good examples of name-calling. In your study indicate your feelings about your findings.

THE USE OF SATIRE

Write a satire of one of the following practices or behaviors in American society.

Over consumption of natural resources, continuing growth of suburbia, the drive to build the tallest skyscraper, our love affair with the automobile, the craving for fast food, gender discrimination, the shopping mall as a social center, the inundation of sexual images in the mass media, the rise in the influence of corporate power over many aspects of life, the amount of time spent before a computer, the high salaries paid to top athletes, the gun culture, the drug culture, the endangered health care system, the escape into virtual reality

REPARTEE

Write an imaginary exchange of sarcastic words between two actual or imaginary characters. Make the exchange of words as sharp and witty as you can. Pretend that the two adversaries are engaged in a verbal archery contest. Share your example with the class.

CHOOSE A SCAPEGOAT

Write down at least two scapegoats for each problem in the following word list:

The failure of the American involvement in Vietnam.

Women's under representation in the seats of political, academic, business and religious power in America.

The persistence of homelessness in America.

The poor performance of American youth in international competitive examinations in science and mathematics.

America's high divorce rate.

Gridlock on America's roadways.

SECTION REVIEW PAPER

Write a propaganda paper for a politician, produce or cause of your choice in which you use at least three of the techniques in this section. At the end of your writing, list the names of the techniques that you have chosen to use.

VOCABULARY BUILDING

Define the following terms used in section 2 and use each term in a sentence: ambiguous, ad hominem, preemptive, non-sequitur, gutter snipe, boondocks, bizarre, "rube goldberg", satire, repartee, scapegoat, Ku Klux Klan

EXERCISES FOR SECTION 3

Practice in using the techniques of Section 3:

APPEAL TO TRADITION

Use this appeal to write in support of any cause of your choice. After this, write another appeal in opposition to any cause of your choice.

DEMAND FOR SPECIAL CONSIDERATION

Write a propaganda paper in support of an affirmative action policy in college and university admissions for the minority group of your choice.

APPEAL TO THE EMOTIONS

Make a written emotional appeal for any political, economic or social cause of your choice. Indicate the emotions you selected for your propaganda paper at the end of your writing.

PERSONIFICATION

Write a paragraph supporting a cause of your choice in which you use the personification technique. After this, write a paragraph attacking a cause of your choice using this technique.

THE USE OF HOT AND COLD WORDS

Expand the listing of offensive terms and their euphemisms that are found in the text under the heading of this technique. Your list should show at least ten items.

LOOK TO THE FUTURE AND BE OPTIMISTIC

Write an optimistic propaganda paper in support of any issue in the following list or, if you wish, write on an issue of your own choosing.

Issue List: the drive for gender equality, race and ethnic relations, ways of controlling violence, space exploration, the future of medical care, the future of education, how to end wars in the world, globalism

LET ALTRUISM REIGN

Write a propaganda paper in support of a philanthropic activity, foundation or organization of your choice. Think of some innovative fund raising techniques.

SECTION REVIEW

Write a propaganda paper for a politician, produce or cause of your choice in which you use at least three of the techniques in this section. At the end of your writing, list the names of the techniques that you have chosen to use.

EXERCISES FOR SECTION 4

Practice in using the techniques of Section 4:

QUOTING OUT OF CONTEXT

Write a quotation out of context. You should research motion picture reviews, political speeches, book reviews, magazine and newspaper articles to obtain original material for your assignment. Write the selected original material and then write a quotation out of context. Put three dot journalism (three dots signify that words have been omitted) to work to distort the meaning that was originally intended by the author or speaker whose statements you are using. Share your work in class.

USE OF NUMBERS TO IMPRESS

Write a propaganda paper publicizing a city, state or nation of your choice in which you list all the superlatives you can find that can be expressed numerically.

Things you might investigate: the number of schools, places of worship, public buildings, parks, playgrounds, growth figures, famous sons and daughters, the number of years since founding, per capita income, life expectancy, annual imports and exports, literacy rate, railway and road mileage, the number of radios, telephones, automobiles, television sets, anything that's big or tall

FALSE DILEMMA

For each of the incomplete dilemmas listed in this exercise supply at least three possible words to complete them:

Example: Elect Cranston for president or race (ruin, four worrisome years, the prospect of a do nothing government).

Fight for your country or

_____

Widen the highway or

_____

Prepare for war or

_____

What will make the statements false dilemmas is to offer only one option when in fact there are more.

USING A MINOR POINT TO DISCREDIT A PERSON, PLACE OR THING

Use a minor point in a paragraph to discredit any person, place or thing of your choice.

LEADING QUESTION

Make up a list of five leading questions you might ask of a person of your choice in an imaginary interview. Be sure that your questions are structured in such a way that they can only be answered with either a yes or no response. Also make sure that regardless of how your questions are answered, the person answering them will be compromised.

SEEK SIMPLE ANSWERS

Choose a politician, product or cause of your choice and write a propaganda paper in which you ask one or more questions designed to illicit a simple answer from your listening or reading audience.

EXAGGERATION OF CONSEQUENCES

Write a propaganda paper that exaggerates the consequences of the passage of a law that you favor. Put a positive spin into your writing. Then, write another propaganda paper that exaggerates the consequences of the passing of a law that you oppose. Put a negative spin into your writing.

DOUBLE TALK

Use double talk in writing a propaganda paper advocating two inconsistent policies at odds with each other.

Possible topics (You may use any of these listed topics or use one of your own choosing.):

Let's keep dangerous substances under control but we must continue to subsidize tobacco growing.

Let's reduce senseless crimes of violence but let's not be too restrictive about the sale of guns.

We need an expanding economy but we must curb growth.
Citizens who are eighteen years old are welcomed into the armed forces and have the right to vote but they must not be allowed to consume alcoholic beverages.

We should spend more on social welfare programs and push forward on my tax cutting proposal.

MANIPULATING NUMBERS

Make a search of the mass media looking for examples of manipulating numbers. Share your findings in class.

BIG LIE

Use the big lie technique to discredit any person, place or thing of your choice. Try searching the mass media for examples of big lies.

PLACEMENT OF EMPHASIS

Use this technique in writing two propaganda papers – one positive and the other negative. For example you could refer to television set ownership in Brazil (year 200 figures) that 34 million Brazilians have television sets. You could also say that 131 million Brazilians don't have television sets.

You may choose a topic from the following topic list:

Airline safety, health insurance in the United States, indoor plumbing in any nation, the number who drowned in the Titanic disaster, % of casualties in the armed forces of the United States in World War II

INNUENDO

Use innuendo in making damaging statements about one topic you'll choose from the following categories:

World leaders, nations of the world, cities of the world, entertainers, music forms, careers. Example: "The city is playing classical music in the town square to get teenagers to vacate the area." The underlying message is that teenagers don't like classical music.

APPEAL TO IGNORANCE

Use this appeal in a propaganda paper attacking the content of any of the programming you select from the mass media.

CARD STACKING

Use card stacking to support any political, economic or social policy, manufactured product or service of your choice in a paragraph. Then use the technique to attack any political, economic or social policy, manufactured product or service of your choice in another paragraph.

STRESS HIGH MORAL PRINCIPLES

Use this technique to support any politician, policy, product or service of your choice.

FALSE URGENCY

Search the mass media for examples illustrating this technique and share your findings in class.

PRAISE ONE THING THE OPPONENT HAS DONE, THEN ON TO THE ATTACK

Use this technique to attack any world leader of your choice. The aim is to seem somewhat fair and balanced in your overall negative assessment of your targeted victim.

MAKE A MINOR CONFESSION AND SAY THAT NOW YOU'VE SEEN THE LIGHT

Choose any one of the following topics in writing an appeal for people to stop the behavior you once might have done yourself.

Topics: excessive drinking of alcoholic beverages, use of curse words, excessive speeding in a car, running red lights, use of illegal drugs, cutting classes in school, being cruel to animals, exhibiting violent behavior, having unprotected sexual relations, vandalizing property

SET UP A STRAW MAN

Use the straw man technique in a propaganda paper opposing any one of the following activities or one of your own choosing:

Activities: building fossil fuel power plants, building vehicles that consume large amounts of fossil fuels, drilling for oil off the coasts of America, American policing of world trouble spots, America's dependence on private transportation; America's stress on building single family housing, the construction of nuclear power plants

TELLING THEM YOU WERE GOING TO LIE BUT COULDN'T DO IT

Use this technique in an imaginary speech on any one of the following subjects or one of your own choosing:

A principal's speech on the future of education presented at a parent-teacher meeting.

A speech to high school students interested in becoming professional athletes.

A speech to medial personnel at a local hospital.

A commercial for any product or service you want to promote.

BUILD A POTEMKIN VILLAGE

Search any real estate advertisements of new developments (in undesirable or inconvenient locations) for signs of "Potemkin villages". Share your findings in class.

Search travel magazines for articles about places that use "Potemkin villages" to present a false impression either cities or countries around the world that want to encourage tourism.

MAKE THE IDEAS BEING SUPPORTED OR OPPOSED SEEM TO BE FORGONE CONCLUSIONS

Use this technique in writing a propaganda paper about a politician or policy of your choice.

DEFINE TERMS TO SUIT GOALS

Use this technique in writing a promotional advertisement for a resort hotel. (Hint: Define exciting getaway in terms that suit your goals.)

SECTION REVIEW PAPER

Write a propaganda paper for a politician, produce or cause in which you use at least three of the techniques from this section. At the end of your writing, list the names of the techniques that you have chosen.

VOCABULARY BUILDING

Define the following terms used in section 4 and use each term in a sentence.

Terms: context, dilemma, innuendo, straw man, Potemkin village, double-talk.

EXERCISES FOR SECTION 5

Practice in using the techniques of Section 5:

APPEAL TO AUTHORITY

Use this technique in writing three statements about each of the following subjects:

Causes you support
Causes you oppose
Products or services you favor
Products or services you don't favor

REPITITION

Choose a product or service you favor and write an advertisement about it using this technique.

USE SLOGANS

Write a slogan of your own making for each of the following subjects:

A candidate for President
A fund raiser for AIDS
A product of your choice
A service of your choice

BANDWAGON

Use this technique in a paragraph in support of a project you'd like to see built in your community, state or nation.

PLAIN FOLKS

Write a public relations paper to make scientists and technicians working for NASA seem like regular fellows and gals.

TRANSFER

Write an advertisement using this technique to encourage young people to use a product or service of your choice.

TESTIMONIAL

Make a list of people you'd use in making testimonial appeals for each of the following products and services. Briefly explain the reasons for your selections in each case.

Products and services:

> stereo systems
> new computers
> women's shoes
> golf clubs
> cruise ship vacations
> cosmetic materials
> an HMO
> dance lessons

USING A BIAS

Write a promotional paper encouraging people to seek the services of an investment company of your choice.

CHALLENGE TO THE EGO

A college or university of your choice wants to increase student enrollment. Use this technique in a promotional paper to catch the attention of high school students.

FLATTERY WILL WORK WONDERS

Use flattery in a propaganda appeal to potential donors to a charity of your choice.

EMPHASIZING CREDENTIALS

Pretend that you are running for the office of student body president at a high school or college. If you don't have any credentials you should make up a few to impress your audience.

TELL THEM IT'S CONFIDENTIAL

Put yourself in the place of a high school math teacher addressing students on the first day of class. You'll tell them confidentially what plans are being discussed for future changes in the curriculum that might affect them. Pledge them to be secretive about this information. If you prefer to be a teacher of another subject other than math, go right ahead.

STIMULATE CURIOSITY

Think of yourself as an alternative energy advocate trying to get people to switch from fossil fuel use to renewable energy sources. Try to get your audience curious about your cause in a one paragraph appeal.

STRUCTURED RESPONSE

Use this technique to persuade people to use any product or service of your choice.

IMITATE, MIMIC OR MOCK THE OPPONENT

Choose any leader of what the United States government describes as a "rogue state" and mock him or her in a paragraph or two.

AD POPULUM

Imagine that you are a speaker going to high schools to inform students about the need to develop safe driving habits. Use popular and current references to connect with your audiences. In other words, play to the gallery!

ACTION INVOLVEMENT

Imagine that you are a high school principal faced with a school that is littered with refuse and graffiti and showing the effects of vandalism. Try to get your student body involved in solving these problems in a speech calling for action.

PRESENT UTOPIAN OR DYSTOPIAN FANTASIES

Imagine yourself as a stockbroker and write a technological utopian fantasy encouraging investors to put their money into a new biotechnology offering.

SCARCITY SELLS

Use this technique in writing an advertisement for any product or service of your choice.

SECTION REVIEW PAPER

Write a propaganda paper for a politician, product, service or cause of your choice in which you use at least three techniques from this section. At the end of your paper, write the names of the techniques that you have used.

BUILDING VOCABULARY

Define the following terms used in section 5 and use each one in a sentence.

Word List: slogan, testimonial, bias, sacred cow, taboo, ego, utopia, dystopia

EXERCISES FOR SECTION 6

Practice in using the techniques of Section 6

SHOCK 'EM

Write just the opening shocking statement of a speech on each of the following topics:

Our Declining Pool of Natural Resources
The World's Population Problem
Marriage Is an Endangered Institution
Plagues Are Coming
Atomic Weapons Are Proliferating
The Scourge of Aids
America's Infrastructure Crisis
The Outlook for World Peace in This Century

THE SHOTGUN APPROACH

For each of the following debate resolutions, list at least five affirmative and five negative arguments:

Resolved: That the Constitution of the United States be amended to allow prayers to be said in public schools.

Resolved: That the Constitution of the United States be amended to make the burning of the American flag a criminal offense.

Resolved: That the voting age be lowered to 16 in federal elections.

Resolved: That capital punishment be prohibited in the United States.

EMPHASIZE ONE POINT

For each of the following debate resolutions, provide what you feel is the strongest affirmative argument and the strongest negative argument:

Resolved: That a national system of medical care for all citizens be established in the United States.

Resolved: That the Electoral College be abolished.

Resolved: That the use of illegal drugs be decriminalized.

Resolved: That English be made the official language of the United States.

BREAK THE ICE

Write at least three jokes or amusing stories that would be good icebreakers to warm up an audience and relieve tensions.

Resolved: That no generating plants powered by nuclear reactors be built in the United States.

Resolved: (any resolution of your choice)

SECTION REVIEW PAPER

Write a propaganda paper for a politician, product or service of your choice in which you use at least three techniques from this section. At the end of your paper, write the names of the techniques you have used.

BUILDING VOCABULARY

Define the following terms used in section 6 and use each term in a sentence:

Word List: Shock, affirmative, resolution (debate). joke, crescendo, emotionalism, proverb, rebut

EXERCISES FOR SECTION 7

Practice in using the techniques of Section 7

USING THE SOCRATIC METHOD

Students should work in pairs to discuss a controversial problem of the day. The discussion should focus on the definitions of key terms that are important to the understanding of the issues involved in the problem. A considerable amount of time should be spent on reaching agreement on definitions even though no overall resolution of the problem may occur.

USE METAPHORS AND SIMILES

Write an appeal in support of a cause of your choice or write a promotional message for any product or service in which you use at least two metaphors or similes. Underline these figures of speech and identify them with a letter *M* for metaphor or with a letter *S* for simile upon completion of your work.

TURN A PROBLEM INTO AN OPPORTUNITY

List five problem situations of your choice. In each case write what you feel would be an appropriate response that would turn the problem into an opportunity to defuse it.

HELP FROM GIANTS OF THE PAST AND PRESENT

Choose a cause, produce, service and person you'd like to support. For each of these subjects search out a quotation from a famous person, past or present, that would be effective in a promotional message for each subject.

TURN A WEAKNESS INTO A STRENGTH

For each of the following hypothetical situations try to turn the weakness into a strength for the person under siege:

A European journalist asks an American high school principal why American students score so low in international science and mathematics examinations. What does the principal say in defense of American secondary education?

A political reporter questions a politician's ability to command given the close election the official barely won. What response does the politician make?

An environmentalist in a discussion with a Detroit automobile executive demands to know why his company continues to produce gas guzzling cars, trucks and vans. How does the executive handle this accusation?

CHOOSE WORDS WISELY

Write to promotional messages for any politician, product, service or cause of your choice. In one message you'll use complex, difficult, obscure or even foreign terms. In the second message you'll rewrite the first message substituting simpler and less obscure terms.

YES, BUT...

Reply to the following statements with a "yes, but..." response:

"Isn't it true that men earn more money than women doing the same work?"

"I hear that you Americans consume more energy than any other people in the world."

I understand that Americans refuse to use the metric system."

SECTION REVIEW PAPER

Write a propaganda paper for a politician, product or cause of your choice in which you use at least three techniques from this section. At the end of your paper, write the names of the techniques you have used.

BUILDING VOCABULARY

Define the following terms used in section 7 and use each one in a sentence:

Word List: Socratic method, metaphor, simile, definition, countermeasure, heckler

BIBLIOGRAPHY

Angell, Norman, Sir *The Public Mind: its disorders, its exploitation* Noel Douglas, London 1926

Beller, E.A. *Propaganda in Germany During The Therty Years War* Princeton Ubiversity Press, 1940

Balfour, Michael Leonard Graham, *Propaganda in War, 1939 – 1945, Organization, Policies and publics in in Britain and Germany* Routledge& Kegan , Boston 1979

Berger, Carl *Broadcasting and Bayonets : the Propaganda War of the American Revolution* University of Pennsylvania Press, Philadelphia 1961

Barghoorn, Frederick Charles *Tne Soviet Image of the United States : a Stud of Distortion* Harcourt Brace , New York 1950

Barson, Michael & Steven Heller *Red Scared! : The Commie Menace in Propaganda and Popular Culture* Chronicle Books, San Francisco 2001

Bergmier, H.J.C. & R.E. Lotz *Hitler's Air Waves: the Inside story of Nazi Radio Broadcasting and Propaganda Swing* Yale University Pres, New Haven, CT 1007

Bernays, Edward *Propaganda* 1 g Publishers Brooklyn, New York 2005

Bredhoff, Stacey *Powers of Persuasion: Poster Art from World War II* National Archives, Washington D.C.

Bradley, Patricia, *Slavery, Propaganda, and the American Revolution*, University of Mississippi Press, Jackson, MI 1999

Bruntz, George G. *Allied Propaganda and the Collapse of the German Empire in 1918* Stanford University Press, Stanford, CA 1938

Cameron, Alan *Claudian: Poetry and Propaganda at the Court of Honorius* Clarendon, Oxford 1970

Causton, Bernard *The Moral Blitz: War Propaganda and Christianity* Secker & Waburg, London 1941

Chandler, Robert W. *War of Ideas: the U.S. Propaganda Campaiagn in Vietnam* Westview Press, Boulder, CO 1981

Chomsky, Noam *Media Control: the Spectacular Achievement of Propaganda*, Seven Stories Press, New York 2002

Charles, Harwood L. ed. *Propaganda by Short WAVE* Princeton University Press, Princeton, NJ 1942

Conason, Joe *Big Lie: The Right- Wing Propaganda Machine and How It Distorts the Truth* St.Martins Press, New York 2003

Cooper, Kent *The Right to Know : an Exposition of the Evils of News Supression and Propaganda* Famar, Straus and Cudahy, New York 1956

Cull, Nicholas John *Selling War : the British Propaganda Campaign Against American Neutrality in World War II* Oxford University Press, New York 1995

De Mendelssohn, Peter *Japan's Political Warfare* G. Allen & Unwin Ltd. London 19444

Doob, Leonard William *Public Opinion and Propaganda* Anchor Books, Hamden, CT 1966

Ducat, Stephen *Takin 1b: American Gullibility and the Reagan Myths* Life Science Press, Tacoma, WA 1988

Dyer, Murray *The Weapons on the Wall : Rethinking Psychological Warfare* Johns Hopkins Press, Baltimore 1959

Elliston, Jon ed. *Psywar on Duba : the Declassified History of U.S. Anti-Castro Propaganda* Ocean Press, New York 1999

Dower, John *Wearing Propaganda : Textiles on the Home Front in Japan , Britain and the United States, 1931 – 1945* Yale University Pres, New Haven 2005

Eisenhower, David *Warwords: U.S. Militarism, the Catholic Right, and the " Bulgarian Connection"* International Publishers, New York 1986

Ettlinger, Harold *The Axis on the Air* the Bobbs – Merrill Co, New York 1943

Edwards, John Carver *Berlin Calling : American Broadcasters in Service to the Third Reich* Praeger, New York 1991

Fawcett, Bill ed. *You Said What : Lies and Propaganda Throughout History* Harper, New York 2007

Foulkes, A. Peter *Literature and Propaganda* Methuem, New York 1983

Fraser, L.M. *Germany Between Two Wars, a Study of Propaganda and War-Guilt* Oxford University Press New York 1945

Gordon, Matthew *News is a Weapon* A.A. Knopf, New York 1942

Grothe, Pete *To Win the Minds of Men : the Story of the Communist Propaganda War in East Germany* Pacific Books, Palo Alto, CA 1964

Gruening, Ernest *The Public Pays : a Study of Power Propaganda* Vanguard Press, New York 1964

Hargrave, John *Propaganda the Mightiest Weapon of All : Words Win Wars* W. Gardner, London 1940

Harvey, Ian *The Techniques of Persuasion : an Essay in Human Relayionships* Falcon Press, London 1951

Herf, Jeffrey *The Jewish Enemy : Nazi Propaganda During World War II Holocaust* Belknap , Cambridge, MA 2008

Holtman, Robert B. *Napoleonic Propaganda* Louisiana State University, Baton Rouge, LA 1950

Honey, Maureen *Creating Rosie the Riveter : Class, Gender, and Propaganda During World War II* University of Massachusetts Press, Amherst 1984

Holt, Robert T. & Robert W. Van de Velde *Strategic Psychological Operations and American Foreign Policy* University of Chicago Press, 1960

Hou, Fu – wu *To Change a Nation : Propaganda and Indoctrination in Communist China* Free Press of Glencoe 1961

Hoyle, Russ *Going to War : How Misinformation , Disinformation, and Propaganda Led America into Iraq* Thomas Dunne Books, New York 2008

Jordan, Weymouth Tyree *Rebels in the Making : Planters, Conventions and Southern Propaganda* Confederate Publishing Co. Tuscaloosa, AL 1958

Joyce, Walter *The Propaganda Gap* Harper Row, New York 1963

Karitzky. Joanne L. *The Mustering of Support for World War I by the Ladies' Home Journal* Edwin Mellen Lewiston, PA 1947

Katz, Daniel Chairman and others ed. *Corporate Aut Society for the Psychological Study of Social Issues , Public Opinion and Propaganda* Dryden Press, New York 1954

Kirkpatrick, Evron M. *Year of Crisis : Communists in Propaganda Activities, 1956* Macmillan, New York 1957

Kominsky, Morris *The Hoaxers : Plain Liars, Fancy Liars. And Damned Liars* Branden Press, Boston 1970

Kurtz, Howard *Spin Cycle : Inside the Clinton Propaganda Machine* Free Press, New York 1998

Lafont, Maria *Soviet Posters : The Sergo Gregorian Collection* Prestel New York 2007

Landsberg, Stefan *Chinese Propaganda Posters : from Revolution to Modernization* Pepin Press, Amsterdam 1995

Laurence, John *The Seeds of Disaster : a Guide to the Realities, race politics, and worldwide Propaganda campaigns of the Republic of South Africa* Taplinger Pub. Co. New York 1968

Lee, Alfred McCung & Elizabeth Briant Lee, ed. *The Fine Artof Propaganda :: A Study of Father Conghlin's Speeches* Harcourt Brace and Co. New York 1939

Lee, John ed. *The Diplomatic Persuaders : the New Role of the Mass Media in International Relations* Wiley, New York 1968

Lee, Thomas F. *Battle babble : Selling Warin America: a Dictionary of Deception* Cimmeron Press, Mobroe, ME

Le, Huu Tri *Prisoner of a Word : a Memoir of the Vietnamese Reeducation Camps* Black Heron Press, Seattle, WA 2001

Lerner, Daniek *Psychological Warfare Against Nazi Germany : The Sykewar Campaign , D-Day to Victory*, MIT Press, Cambridge, MA 1971

Lowenthal, Leo *Prophets of Deceit : a Study of the Techniques of the American Agitator* Harper, New York 1949

Mac Arthur, John R. *Second Front : Censorship and Propaganda in the Gulf War* HILL AND Wang, New York 1992

Mac Kenzie, John M. *Propaganda and Empire : the Manipulation of British Public Opinion, 1880 – 1960* Manchester University Press 1984

Manning, J. & Herbert Romerstein *Historical Dictionary of American Propaganda* Greenwood Press, West Point, CN 2004

Martin, John L. *International Propaganda : its Legal and Diplomatic Control* University of Minnesota Press, Minneapolis 1958

Mock, James R. *Words That Won the War – the Story of the Committee on Public Information, 1917 – 1919* Princeton University Press, Princeton, NJ 1939

Moore, Albert L. *Postal Propaganda of the Third Reich* Schiffer Military History , Atglen, PA 2003

Murty, B.S. *Propaganda and World Public Order : the Legal Regulation of the Ideological Instrument of Coertion* Yale University Press, New Haven, CN 1968

Osgood, Kenneth Alan *Total Cold War : Eisenhower's Secret Propaganda Battle at Home and Abroad* University of Kansas Press, Lawrence, KS 2006

Page, Caroline *U.S. Official Propaganda During the Vietnam War, 1965 – 1973 : the Limits of Persuasion* Leicester University Press, New York 1996

Parfrey, Adam ed. *Extreme Islam: Anti-American Propaganda of Muslim Fundamentalists* Feral House , Los Angeles, CA 2001

Penny, L. *Your Call is Important to Us : The Truth About Bullshit* Crown Publishers, New York 2005

Peterson, H.C. *Propaganda for War : the Campaign Against American Neutrality 1914 – 1917* University of Oklahoma Press, Norman 1939

Perris, Arnold *Music as Propaganda : Art to Prtsuade, and to Control* Greenwood Press, Westport, CN 1995

Ppowell, David E. *Antireligious Propaganda in the Soviet Union: A Study of Mass Persuasion* The MIT Press, Cambridge, MA 1975

Pratkanis, Anthony R. *Age of Propaganda : the Everyday Use and Abuse of Persuasion* W.H. Freeman, New York 1992

Rampton, Sheldon *The Best War Ever : Lies, Damned Lies and the Mess in Iraq* Penguin, New York 2006

Rampton, Sheldon *Weapons of Mas Deception : the Uses of Propaganda in Bush's War on Iraq* Penguin, New York 2003

Rich, Frank *The Greatest Story Ever Sold : the Decline and Fall of Truth from 9/11 to Katrina* Penguin Press, New York 2006

Rhodes, Anthony *Propaganda : the Art of Persuasion ; World War II* Chelsea House Publishers, New York 1976

Roeder, George H. *The Censored War : American Visual Experience During World War II* Yale University Press, New Haven, CN 1993

Roetter, Charles *The Art of Psychological Warfare, 1914 – 1945* Stein and Day, New York 1974

Snyder, Alvin A. *Warriors of Disinformation : American Propaganda , Soviet Lies, and the Winning of the Cold War* Arcade Publishers, New York 1995

Soley, Lawrence C. *Radio Warfare : OSS and CIA Subversive Propaganda* Praeger, New York, 1989

Sorensen, Thomas C. *The Word War: the Story of American Propaganda* Harper & Row , New York 1968

Summers, Robert E. *America's Weapons of Psychological Warfare* Wilson, New York 1951

Szanto, Andres *What Orwell didn't Know: Propaganda, the New Face of American Politics* Public Affairs, New York 2007

Teyllor, Richard **Film Propaganda : Soviet Russia and Nazi Germany Barnes & Noble Booke, New York 1979**

Thomson, Oliver **Mass Persuasion in History : an Historical Analysis of the Development of Propaganda Techniques Crane, Russak, New York 1977**

Thum,, Gladys & Marcells Thum **The Persuaders : Propaganda in War and Peace Atheneum, New York 1972**

Tran, Tri Vu *Lost Years : My 1,632 Days in VIETNAMESE Reeducation Camps* Institute of East Asian Studies, University of California, Berkeley 1988

Wheeler, Marey *Anatomy of Deceit : How yhe Bush Administration Used the Media to Sell the Iraq War and Out a Spy* Vasten Books, New York 2007

Wiegand, Wayne A. *An Active Investment for Propaganda : the American Public Library During World War I*

Wilkerson, Marcus Manley *Public Opinion and the Spanish American War: a Study in War Propaganda* Russell and Russell, New York 1967

Wright, Micah Ian *You Back the Attack! We'll Bomb Who We Want! : Remixed War Propaganda* Steven Stories Press, New York 2003

Yu, Frederick T. *News Persuasion in Communist China* Praeger, New York 1964

Zeman, Z. A.B. *Selling the War : Art and Propaganda in World War II* Exeter Books, New York 1982

www.ingramcontent.com/pod-product-compliance
Lightning Source LLC
Chambersburg PA
CBHW061246280526
45784CB00002B/659